TROUT FLIES OF THE EAST

TROUT FLIES
OF THE EAST

Best Contemporary Patterns
from East of the Rockies

JIM SCHOLLMEYER
and **TED LEESON**

Frank
Amato
PORTLAND

All inquiries should be addressed to:
Frank Amato Publications, Inc.
P.O. Box 82112 • Portland, Oregon 97282 • 503-653-8108
www.amatobooks.com

Book Design: Amy Tomlinson
Photography: Jim Schollmeyer

Printed in Hong Kong
1 3 5 7 9 10 8 6 4 2

Softbound ISBN: 1-57188-196-4   Softbound UPC: 0-66066-00407-9
Spiral Hardbound ISBN: 1-57188-197-2   Spiral Hardbound UPC: 0-66066-00408-6

TABLE OF
CONTENTS

Introduction

The enormous growth in fly fishing seems, at times, to have brought with it a certain standardization and uniformity. Most types of tackle are distributed nationwide; fishermen across the country routinely trade ideas; and fly anglers from coast to coast now arrive streamside with much the same equipment and technical information. But some elements of fly fishing remain unique and individual, and to find them we need look no further than the assortment of artificial flies in nearly any fly shop. There in the bins, among dozens of standard and familiar patterns, are a handful of flies designed and tied by knowledgeable local anglers for use on waters in the area. They are the "shop patterns," the house favorites, the flies you won't find anywhere else, and far more often than not, they are the top choices for fishing rivers and lakes in a given area. In fly fishing, there's no substitute for local knowledge.

Trout Flies of the East is one of a series of books devoted to presenting these local patterns to a larger audience of tyers. Like its companion volumes, *Trout Flies of the West* and *Inshore Flies: Contemporary Patterns from the Atlantic and Gulf Coasts,* this book is intended in part as a resource for anglers who live in or will travel to a particular region of the country and wish to equip themselves with proven patterns. But as most fishermen know, good fly patterns travel well, and an imitation designed for a particular area or specific river may well be equally effective on waters in other parts of the country. A new idea, a new design may be the answer when more conventional patterns fail—particularly on hard-fished waters where trout grow accustomed to seeing the same flies presented day after day and are more likely to respond with a yawn than a strike. Whether general attractors, hatch-matching patterns, or imitations of the many aquatic food forms, the flies shown here can provide trout anglers everywhere with a fresh approach on familiar waters and new ones.

To compile this book, we contacted fly shops east of the Rocky Mountains and asked them to contribute patterns designed for their local streams and lakes. The response was both enthusiastic and generous, with nearly 80 shops from 25 states and provinces submitting over 400 patterns; they include spring creek patterns of the Upper Midwest, freestone flies for streams of the Southeast, hatch-matching patterns from storied waters of the Mid-Atlantic states, smelt and baitfish imitations from New England, brook trout patterns from Newfoundland and Ontario, and just about everything in between. Taken together, they represent the enormous wealth of ingenuity and skill that is to be found among local tyers throughout North America.

About This Book

To make this book as useful as possible to tyers, we have shown many of the flies from more than one angle since the simple side-view customarily used in pattern books does not always provide the kind of detail necessary to reproduce a fly at the vise. For each pattern, the main photograph (on a green background) generally pictures the fly in profile; supplementary photos (on a blue background) show selected patterns from the top, underside, and/or front as a way of illustrating more clearly the proportions, placement, or arrangement of material on the hook shank. In some cases, these supplementary photos show alternate colors, color combinations, or materials recommended by the originator or tyer. Similarly, the "Comments" section that accompanies the pattern may contain brief instructions from the tyers themselves about dressing the pattern or some of its less-familiar components.

And because tying a fly is really the starting point, rather than the endpoint, of fishing, the "Comments" sections frequently contain information from the tyer or contributing shop about where, how, or under what circumstances the fly can be fished most effectively.

For convenient reference, we've divided the patterns into categories that correspond to certain fly types. This kind of grouping is at best an uncertain and imprecise business since a great number of patterns tend to cross boundaries. Take, for example, the Muddler Minnow and its many variations. This very same fly could be used to imitate a sculpin or other baitfish, a large adult stonefly, a grasshopper, and in appropriate sizes and colors, a hellgrammite, stonefly nymph, or adult caddis. Or consider the Woolly Bugger, perhaps one of the most widely used fly styles today; depending on how, when, or where it's fished, it can imitate a leech, sculpin or baitfish, stonefly nymph, damselfly nymph, or even a crayfish. In short, consigning a given fly pattern to a single representational category is, at times, an almost arbitrary matter. In categorizing the flies, we've been guided by information provided by the contributors, and when a fly has multiple imitative purposes, these are listed. But we suggest that readers seeking a particular type of pattern (a grasshopper, for instance) browse through other sections of the book (stoneflies, caddisflies, general attractors, for example) where they may find a fly that fills the bill.

About the Flies

The patterns in this book are all designed primarily for trout fishing, though again such boundaries are not easily fixed. Some flies are well-suited to steelhead, salmon, or warmwater species, and such applications may be briefly mentioned in the accompanying comments. But the central focus here is on trout patterns.

Since there is an entry under each pattern for the "originator" of the fly, a word of explanation is in order. Some patterns in this book are variations of more familiar fly styles. In such cases, we have listed the "originator" as the tyer who devised the specific version that is pictured, with the understanding that most tyers will recognize the fly as an adaptation of a well-know design—as a variation of Al Caucci and Bob Nastasi's Comparadun, for instance (itself a version of an earlier Fran Betters design) or of Frank Sawyer's Pheasant Tail nymph. And in fact many of the submitting shops and tyers strongly emphasized that their patterns were variations rather than wholly original designs. As many of the tyers pointed out to us, the originator of pattern can be difficult to determine, since fly patterns tend to evolve continually. Except for those patterns of unknown origin, however, we have credited an originator to each fly as a way of acknowledging either a tyer's adaptation of an existing design or, as is the case with many of the patterns shown here, a tyer's largely original dressing.

It is worth pointing out that some of the flies in this book, especially those designed to imitate particular insects such as a mayfly dun or caddis pupa, are really fly designs rather than specific patterns. That is, by altering the hook size and colors of materials, you can use the same basic fly style to imitate a variety of species. Thus while a fly pictured in these pages may represent a sulphur emerger, for example, or a *Baetis* dun, the same basic design can be adapted to represent a March brown, green drake, and so on. Similarly, many patterns can be used to represent different insects; the same fly may be successful during a caddis, mayfly, or midge hatch. In many instances, the contributing shop or tyer has indicated in the "Comments" section that such adaptations of the pattern are both common and recommended. Again, browsing through different sections of the book is the best way of identifying the range of uses for the flies shown.

In the recipes that accompany each pattern, some tyers have been emphatic about the use of specific materials—the particular location on a pheasant skin of the feather used for hackling, or a particular brand and shade of synthetic body material. Other tyers have been less insistent on such matters, merely identifying a material as, say, "olive dubbing." Readers, of course, are free to substitute or alter materials as they choose, but those seeking to reproduce as closely as possible the pattern as it is pictured may at times run into some less commonly available materials, or trade names (particularly in the growing area of synthetic materials) that are not familiar. In almost every case, the contributing shops can provide information about the patterns, sample flies, and the materials used to dress them. These shops are listed in a directory at the end of the book. A large number of them can also assist in arranging guides, casting instruction, float trips in some cases, and other destination services, and they are a useful resource for anglers traveling throughout the eastern and southern United States and Canada.

Finally, we would like to extend our deepest thanks to the shops and tyers who generously shared their patterns, tying techniques, information, and enthusiasm for this project. Designing effective fly patterns often requires significant time, experimentation, and persistence, and we are grateful to the tyers who gave us the benefit of their experience. They had the hard part of writing this book.

CHAPTER **1**

General Attractor and Multi-Purpose Flies

Dry Flies

Arrowhead

Alternate version with counterwrapped fine copper wire

Pattern type: General attractor
Submitted by: Perry's Trout Fly Shop (Duluth, Minnesota)
Originated by: Earl Grummett
Tied by: Perry A. Rowlison
Alternate version:
Submitted by: The Superior Fly Angler (Superior, Minnesota)
Tied by: Matt Paulson

Hook: 3XF, #10
Thread: Black 6/0
Tail: One grizzly and one brown hackle tip, tied split
Body: Peacock herl reinforced with tying thread
Ribbing: Hackles from tails palmered over body

Comments: "Arrowhead" refers to the Arrowhead Region of northeastern Minnesota. Tyer Perry Rowlison fishes this fly on the leader point with a Duzzie (p. 23) as the dropper. The Arrowhead should be bounced on the surface.

Avery Creek Parachute

Comments: "This fly," explains Henry Williamson, "is normally fished on small Appalachian freestone streams where the trout are small or not selective, but they do seem to respond to bright colors. The originator of the pattern was Jack Cabe, who now fishes the streams we mortals have yet to wade."

Pattern type: General attractor
Submitted by: The Fish Hawk, Inc. (Atlanta, Georgia)
Originated by: Jack Cabe
Tied by: Henry Williamson

Hook: TMC 100, #12-#16
Thread: Orange UNI 8/0
Tail: Ginger hackle fibers
Body: Orange dubbing
Wing: White Antron
Hackle: Brown Hoffman saddle

Brookie Cookie

Pattern type: General attractor
Submitted by: The Sporting Gentleman (Media, Pennsylvania)
Originated by: Tom Fink
Tied by: Tom Fink

Hook: Mustad 94842, #14
Thread: Orange UNI 6/0
Tail: Red rooster spade hackle, tied long
Body: Peacock herl from near feather eye
Ribbing: Orange tying thread
Hackle: Grizzly saddle, wrapped with shiny side toward hook eye

Comments: This fly is fished primarily in high-elevation brook-trout streams.

Coachman Betty

Pattern type: General attractor
Submitted by: Backcast Fly Shop (Benzonia, Michigan)
Originated by: unknown
Tied by: Jim Empie

Hook: Mustad 94840 or TMC 101, #6-#12
Thread: Black
Tail: Red duck quill fibers, hackle fibers, or calf tail
Body: Peacock herl with red floss band
Wing: White calf tail
Hackle: Brown

Comments: This fly was developed for brook trout fishing in the Michigan's Upper Peninsula. It is a good attractor pattern that can be fished either wet or dry.

Confetti Fly

Front view

Pattern type: General attractor
Submitted by: Severn Wharf Custom Rods (Gloucester Point, Virginia)
Originated by: R.B. Mays
Tied by: R.B. Mays

Hook: Dry fly, #8-#18
Thread: Yellow UNI-Stretch, 1X
Tag: Tying thread
Tail: Rainbow Krystal Flash (#13)
Body: Fluorescent green tinsel chenille, medium
Ribbing: Holographic tinsel
Wings: Yellow Antron
Hackle: Gray emu feathers (white for white version)

Comments: This pattern deliberately incorporates as few natural materials as possible and was designed for brook trout fishing in the Blue Ridge Mountains of Virginia. Use plenty of floatant.

White-hackle version

Dark Humpy

Pattern type: General attractor
Submitted by: Corey's Handtied Flies (Yarmouth, Nova Scotia)
Originated by: Graden LeBlanc
Tied by: Corey Burke

Hook: Mustad 94840, #10-#14
Thread: Brown
Tail: Deer hair
Body: Peacock herl
Shellback: Deer hair from tail
Hackle: Brown

Comments: Originator Graden LeBlanc was a local Nova Scotia tyer who supplied many lodges with flies. He devised this version of the Humpy which is popular in both Nova Scotia and Newfoundland.

F-C Crackleback

Pattern type: General attractor, terrestrial, diving caddis
Submitted by: Feather-Craft Fly Fishing (St. Louis, Missouri)
Originated by: Ed Story
Tied by: Ed Story

Hook: Dai-Riki 300, #12
Thread: Olive UNI 8/0
Body: PMD dubbing or turkey round PMD
Shellback: Peacock herl
Hackle: Furnace saddle

Comments: Ed Story devised this pattern in 1955. It can be fished dry as a terrestrial imitation or skipped subsurface as a diving caddis.

Floating Squirrel

Pattern type: General attractor
Submitted by: Northern Tier Outfitters (Galeton, Pennsylvania)
Originated by: Brad Bireley
Tied by: Brad Bireley

Hook: Daiichi 1180, #10-#18
Thread: Chartreuse 8/0
Shuck: Tan Spirit River Sparkle Yarn
Body: Gray Squirrel/SLF dubbing
Wing: Hareline fluorescent chartreuse Para Post
Hackle: Grizzly

Comments: Brad Bireley notes, "This is a great "go-to" fly when nothing is hatching. You can vary body and shuck colors, but this particular combination works great."

Houghton Lake Special

Pattern type: General attractor
Submitted by: Dan's Fly Shop (Roscommon, Michigan)
Originated by: Jack Schwiegert
Tied by: Dan Rivard

Hook: 4XL, #1-#10
Thread: Black size A or E, or Kevlar
Tail: Red yarn, one hook gap in length
Body: Black acrylic yarn or chenille
Ribbing: Oval silver tinsel
Wing: Brown bucktail over white bucktail
Hackle: 3or 4 brown hackles for #1-#4;
2 or 3 brown hackles for #6-#10

Comments: Dan Rivard notes, "Tie this fly on after midnight and use at least 1x tippet, heavier is better. A 7-foot leader is okay, but 9 or 10 feet will absorb the shock of the strike better. DO NOT reach/fumble for a smoke while allowing the fly to sit unless you enjoy losing your smokes, lighter, rod, reel, and line—instead, pay attention!" He advises dressing the wing with as much bucktail as you can without breaking the tying thread. The brown bucktail makes up 1/4 of the total wing; white bucktail makes up the remainder.

Improved Yellow Adams

Front view

Pattern type: General attractor
Submitted by: South Mountain Custom Rod & Tackle
(Lebanon, Pennsylvania)
Originated by: Jim Yurejefcic
Tied by: Jim Yurejefcic

Hook: Dry fly, #12-#18
Thread: Black 8/0
Tail: Grizzly hackle fibers
Body: Round yellow closed-cell foam
Wings: Grizzly hackle tips
Hackle: Grizzly

Comments: Jim Yurejefcic explains, "The original of this pattern was given to me by Dave Wolf. He had tied the fly using yellow dubbing as a body material. The closed-cell foam was added to give floatability to the fly. When tying this pattern, we use a round foam, which gives a segmented effect to the body."

Jim's Retriever

Front view

Pattern type: General attractor
Submitted by: South Mountain Custom Rod & Tackle
(Lebanon, Pennsylvania)
Originated by: Jim Yurejefcic
Tied by: Jim Yurejefcic

Hook: Mustad 94840, #12-#18
Thread: Dark brown 8/0
Tail: Brown grizzly hackle fibers
Body: Underfur from golden retriever
Wings: Brown grizzly hackle tips
Hackle: Barred ginger

Comments: "This fly started out as a joke," notes Jim Yurejefcic, "when my wife came home with two golden retriever puppies. But we found out it really takes trout. If you don't have a golden retriever, you can substitute any dubbing that's two or three shades darker than a light Cahill. Although this pattern is an attractor, it will take fish during the light Cahill hatch."

Lenexa Special

Pattern type: General attractor
Submitted by: Severn Wharf Custom Rods (Gloucester Point, Virginia)
Originated by: Richard Hines
Tied by: Richard Hines

Hook: Dry fly, #12-#20
Thread: Black 12/0
Tail: Moose body hair
Body: March brown Antron dubbing
Ribbing: 3 strands chartreuse Supreme Hair, twisted
Wings: Yellow calf body
Hackle: Brown

Comments: "This fly," notes Richard Hines, "shows up well on the water because of its yellow wings. It can easily be tied down to size 18. The Lenexa Special floats well and holds up to hard fishing; the rib seems to protect the body dubbing. In larger sizes, #10, it is a good bluegill fly."

Mr. Ed

Pattern type: General attractor
Submitted by: Severn Wharf Custom Rods (Gloucester Point, Virginia)
Originated by: Richard Hines
Tied by: Richard Hines

Hook: Dry fly, #12-#20
Thread: Black 12/0
Tails: Grizzly and brown hackle fibers, mixed
Abdomen: Black horse hair (from back)
Wing: Orange calf body
Thorax: Sulphur orange dubbing
Hackle: Grizzly and brown

Comments: The orange wing makes this pattern highly visible, even in broken water. Tyer Richard Hines notes that black quill could probably be substituted for horse hair on this pattern.

P.B. Skater Yellow

Pattern type: General attractor, stonefly
Submitted by: Hair & Things Guide Service and Fly Shop (Rutland, Vermont)
Originated by: Paul R. Buccheri
Tied by: Paul R. Buccheri

Hook: Daiichi 1130, #10
Thread: Red UNI 8/0
Body: Peacock herl underbody; yellow poly yarn or foam mounted at rear and pulled forward on underside of shank for bottom of body
Ribbing: Gold wire
Hackle: 2 ginger hackles palmered, with dull side forward

Comments: Paul Buccheri fishes this fly by quartering upstream, raising the rod to make a 70-degree angle with the water, and stripping line slowly; the belly of the line pulls the fly and skates it across the surface. This is an effective pattern during stonefly hatches on the Androscoggin and Connecticut rivers.

Riffle Fly

Pattern type: General attractor, mayfly dun
Submitted by: North Country Angler (Intervale, New Hampshire)
Originated by: Dick Surette
Tied by: Bill Thompson

Hook: Mustad 9671, #10-#12
Thread: Black
Tail: White calf tail
Body: Gray muskrat dubbing
Wings: White calf tail (tied twice the normal height)
Hackle: 3 grizzly

Comments: Bill Thompson notes, "Tied in the 1960s by Dick Surette, founder of North Country Angler, the Riffle Fly is meant to be used at dusk in fast water. The calf tail wings are tied oversize to increase visibility. The body color is sometimes changed, but wings and tail are always white."

River Ranger

Pattern type: General attractor
Submitted by: The Forks Fly Shop (Inglewood, Ontario)
Originated by: Wayne F. Martin
Tied by: Wayne F. Martin

Hook: TMC 103 BL, #17
Thread: White for body, black for head
Tail: Brown deer hair
Underbody: Double layer of yellow nylon rod-building thread or yellow floss
Shellback: White deer hair
Thorax: Olive Fly-Rite dubbing
Wing: Snowshoe rabbit foot guard hair tied fan style
Hackle: Dark reddish-brown rooster hackle

Comments: Wayne Martin points out that the tendency is to overdress this fly—too much material, too many thread wraps. Keep it sparse. This pattern should float high. Use a dry-powder floatant and dead-drift or skate the fly in fast or slow water.

West Branch Adams

Pattern type: General attractor, mayfly or caddis
Submitted by: Beaver Kill Angler (Roscoe, New York)
Originated by: David E. Pabst
Tied by: David E. Pabst

Hook: Mustad 94840, #10-#20
Thread: Pale olive 6/0
Tail: Cree hackle fibers
Body: Yellowish-green rabbit fur dubbing
Wings: Grizzly hackle tips
Hackle: Brown and grizzly mixed

White River Dog Fly

Pattern type: General attractor
Submitted by: Sodie's (St. George, Kansas)
Originated by: Craig Phillips
Tied by: Craig Phillips

Hook: TMC 900BL or standard dry-fly, #10-#16
Thread: Tan UNI 6/0, or color to match body
Tail: Grizzly saddle hackle fibers
Body: Long hairs from Great Pyrenees or other long-haired dog
Ribbing (opt.): Fine copper wire
Hackle: Grizzly saddle hackle

Comments: Craig Phillips explains, "I first tied this fly several years ago when I began tying. I had only cheap saddle hackles, so I used them for the tail and hackle. I believe that the lower-quality hackle allows the fly to ride low in the water, giving it a slightly different profile to the fish. The body material can be obtained by brushing any long-haired dog. I do not dub the hair, but create a 'rope' by rolling it in my hands. I then tie the rope in at the back of the fly and wrap it forward.

Since the original version, shown here, I have tied this fly with hackle tip and calf tail wings, reverse "Waterwisp" style, and a dark version tied with Irish Setter hair. I fish the white version in bright light, and switch to the dark one near evening or very early in the morning. This pattern made its debut on the White River in Arkansas and has been effective as well in Colorado and Wisconsin."

Nymphs

A.J.F. Ostrich BH Nymph

Pattern type: General attractor
Submitted by: The Camp-Site (Huntington Station, New York)
Originated by: Amedeo J. Forzano
Tied by: Amedeo J. Forzano

Hook: Mustad 9671, #12
Thread: Black 6/0
Tail: Pink marabou
Body: Black ostrich herl twisted with round gold tinsel, wrapped
Head: Brass bead

Comments: This pattern is also effective with an orange or yellow tail.

Bead Head Brule River Pheasant Tail

Pattern type: General attractor
Submitted by: The Superior Fly Angler (Superior, Wisconsin)
Originated by: Jeff Dahl
Tied by: Matt Paulson

Hook: Mustad 9671, #6-#14
Thread: Black 6/0
Tail: Pheasant tail fibers
Body: Pheasant tail fibers
Ribbing: Fine copper wire, counterwrapped
Wing case: Pheasant tail fibers
Legs: Hen saddle palmered over thorax
Head: Copper bead

Top view

Front view

Bead-Head Micro

Pattern type: General attractor
Submitted by: Park Place Exxon (Richwood, West Virginia)
Originated by: Oak Myers
Tied by: Oak Myers

Hook: Mustad 80200BR, #12-#16
Thread: Olive 6/0 Flymaster
Tail: Peacock herl
Body: Peacock Micro-cable
Collar: Spirit River Nymph Blend, peacock
Head: 3/32" brass bead

Comments: This pattern, notes tyer Oak Myers, is quick and easy to tie, and extremely durable.

Bob's Bead Head Flashback Strip Nymph

Pattern type: General attractor
Submitted by: Bob Mitchell's Fly Shop (Lake Elmo, Minnesota)
Originated by: Tracy Peterson
Tied by: Tracy Peterson

Hook: TMC 5263, #8; strip of lead wire lashed along top of shank so hook rides point-up
Thread: Brown or tan 6/0
Tail: Bleached fox fur with 4 strands pearl Flashabou
Body: Fox squirrel spun in dubbing loop
Shellback: Pearl Flashabou
Ribbing: Fine copper wire
Thorax: Grizzly hen neck hackle and fox squirrel spun in dubbing loop, palmered
Head: 3/16" brass bead

Top view

Char-shenk Special Nymph

Pattern type: General attractor
Submitted by: South Mountain Custom Rod & Tackle (Lebanon, Pennsylvania)
Originated by: David R. Shenk
Tied by: David R. Shenk

Hook: Mustad AC80250BR or TMC 2487, #10-#14
Thread: Chartreuse UNI-Stretch nylon
Tail: Chartreuse UNI-Stretch, frayed
Body: Chartreuse UNI-Stretch, built up by wrapping back and forth across shank
Ribbing: Clear V-Body Glass
Wing: Chartreuse Gherke's Fish Fuzz
Head: Gold metal bead

Comments: This pattern was originally designed as an emerger/nymph, but has proven effective as a general attractor.

Crystal Egg Pheasant Tail Nymph

Pattern type: Mayfly or stonefly nymph carrying egg
Submitted by: Eldredge Bros. Fly Shop (Cape Neddick, Maine)
Originated by: Travis Johnson
Tied by: Travis Johnson

Hook: TMC 2457, #10
Thread: Olive UNI 6/0
Tail: 6 pheasant tail fibers
Abdomen: Pheasant tail fibers
Wing case: Pheasant tail fibers
Thorax: Umpqua Glo-Brite Chenille, orange, pink, or red

Comments: This is a good fall/winter pattern; it should be fished dead drift close to the bottom.

Crystal Wiggler

Pattern type: General attractor
Submitted by: Backcast Fly Shop (Benzonia, Michigan)
Originated by: Ben Forrester
Tied by: Ben Forrester

Hook: Mustad 9672, #6-#8
Thread: Black
Tail: Gray squirrel tail
Body: Black opalescent Estaz
Shellback: Gray squirrel hair from tail

Top view

Comments: This pattern can be dressed with various colors of Estaz or tinsel chenille.

Dancing Devil

Pattern type: General attractor
Submitted by: Fly and Field (Glen Ellyn, Illinois)
Originated by: Dennis Graupe
Tied by: Dan Grant

Hook: TMC 3761, #14
Thread: Black
Tail: Red Hareline Micro Ultra Chenille
Body: Peacock herl
Legs: Red Hareline Micro Ultra Chenille

Top view

Comments: This pattern fishes best when the legs are all askew. It is used extensively in the spring creeks of southwest Wisconsin. Add weight to the fly to get it deep. The tail and legs are tapered to a point with a lighter.

Deluxe Peacock

Pattern type: General attractor
Submitted by: Fly and Field (Glen Ellyn, Illinois)
Originated by: Steve Fanelli
Tied by: Steve Fanelli

Hook: Partridge G1 Single Wilson Hook, #16
Thread: Black UNI 8/0
Tail: 4 blue peacock body feather fibers
Body: Peacock herl, trimmed to taper toward rear
Wing case: Gold peacock back feathers coated with Flexament
Legs: Blue peacock body feather fibers, tied beard style

Comments: "This fly," says Steve Fanelli, "was designed around the premise that if a little peacock is good, a lot of peacock is great. This is a great all-round searching pattern."

Forrester's Frenzy

Pattern type: General attractor
Submitted by: Backcast Fly Shop (Benzonia, Michigan)
Originated by: Ben Forrester
Tied by: Ben Forrester

Hook: Mustad 3906, #8-#10; weighted with lead wire
Thread: Black or dark brown
Body: Cream dubbing (light yellow yarn for light yellow version)
Ribbing: Silver tinsel (gold for light yellow version)
Shellback: Turkey quill
Hackle: Brown

Light yellow version

Comments: This pattern should be fished deep.

Golden Flashback Nymph

Pattern type: General attractor
Submitted by: Choo Choo Fly & Tackle (Chattanooga, Tennessee)
Originated by: Brad Weeks
Tied by: Brad Weeks

Hook: TMC 3761, #12; weighted with .025" lead wire on front half of shank and flattened
Thread: Light Cahill 6/0
Tail: Wood duck flank fibers
Abdomen: Red squirrel belly
Thorax: Red squirrel back
Ribbing: Fine oval tinsel
Wing case: Flat gold tinsel, extra wide

Top view

Great White Hope

Pattern type: General attractor
Submitted by: The Sporting Tradition (Lexington, Kentucky)
Originated by: Dewayne Holder
Tied by: Rob Fightmaster

Hook: TMC 2457, #12-#16
Thread: Gray 6/0
Tail: Pheasant tail fibers
Body: Pearl green Lite Brite
Shellback: Gray Scud Back
Ribbing: Monofilament
Head: Gold metal bead

Comments: Tyer Rob Fightmaster explains, "We're not really sure what this is supposed to be: caddis, scud, sow-bug? Whatever it is, it catches fish. Dewayne designed this fly to be fished on the Cumberland River tailwater, where it is a killer. We have since enjoyed the fly's success on numerous other tailwaters as well as many mountain streams in eastern Kentucky, Tennessee, and North Carolina."

Hester's Woolly Stone

Pattern type: General attractor
Submitted by: Chesapeake Fly & Bait Company (Arnold, Maryland)
Originated by: Jim Hester
Tied by: Jim Hester

Hook: Mustad 9671 or Mustad 9672, #8-#12; weight (optional) several wraps fine lead wire
Thread: Tan Danville Flymaster 6/0
Tail: Brown with copper sparkle Sili-Legs
Body: Peacock herl
Ribbing: Olive grizzly saddle hackle, palmered over body
Legs: Brown with copper sparkle Sili-Legs
Head: Tan rabbit fur dubbing or hare's ear blend
Antennae: Brown with copper sparkle Sili-Legs

Comments: Jim Hester notes that this pattern, which began as a smallmouth bass fly, is now his favorite searching pattern for trout.

Jim's All Purpose Nymph (Olive)

Pattern type: General attractor
Submitted by: Chesapeake Fly & Bait Company (Arnold, Maryland)
Originated by: Jim Hester
Tied by: Jim Hester

Hook: Mustad 9671 or Mustad 9672, #8-#14; weighted with fine lead wire
Thread: Black Danville Flymaster 6/0
Tail: Olive marabou
Body: Dark olive rabbit fur dubbing with guard hairs left in
Ribbing: Fine pearl Mylar tinsel
Wing case: Olive marabou fibers
Legs: Dubbing picked out
Head: Peacock herl

Krystal Pupa

Pattern type: General attractor
Submitted by: Dakota Angler & Outfitter (Rapid City, South Dakota)
Originated by: Jim Smoragiewicz
Tied by: Jim Smoragiewicz

Hook: Partridge K4A, Daiichi 1150, or TMC 2487, #16-#20
Thread: Olive Benecchi 12/0
Tail: Pheasant tail fibers
Abdomen: Pearl Krystal Flash
Wing case: Pearl Krystal Flash
Thorax: Arizona Peacock dubbing
Head: Clear glass bead

Comments: "This fly," notes Jim Smoragiewicz, "is a great mid-winter attractor pattern when fish are taking midge pupae."

Nympho

Top view (version with fuchsia thorax

Pattern type: General attractor
Submitted by: River's Edge Fly Shop (Thunder Bay, Ontario)
Originated by: Scott E. Smith
Tied by: Scott E. Smith

Hook: TMC 200R or Daiichi 1270, #8-#10
Thread: Orange UNI 6/0
Tail: Golden pheasant crest
Abdomen: Chartreuse Steelhead Dubbin
Ribbing: Gold oval tinsel
Wing case: 6 strands peacock herl
Thorax: Orange or fuchsia Steelhead Dubbin
Legs: Fibers of thorax dubbing picked out

Comments: Tyer Scott Smith notes that this fly is tied to the same proportions as the standard Gold Ribbed Hare's Ear Nymph.

Peacock Wooly Worm

Pattern type: General attractor, damselfly nymph
Submitted by: The Fish Hawk, Inc. (Atlanta, Georgia)
Originated by: unknown
Tied by: Henry Williamson

Hook: TMC 3761, #12-#16; weighted with .010" or .015" lead wire covered with olive tying thread
Thread: Olive UNI 8/0
Body: 5-6 strands peacock herl
Hackle: Brown Hoffman saddle
Head: Gold bead ahead of red thread band

Comments: Tyer Henry Williamson explains, "This fly was shown to me in the 1970s by Bob Martin of Greenville, South Carolina. He learned it from a guide in Island Park, Idaho in the 1960s. The locals out here fish it dead drift, nymph style, in moving water or strip it streamer style in stillwater. This fly is a big-time favorite among the old-time fly fishers of our area. Without fail, this fly produces my biggest fish, year after year—can't say enough about this pattern."

Razor Back

Pattern type: General attractor
Submitted by: Fly and Field (Glen Ellyn, Illinois)
Originated by: Steve Fanelli
Tied by: Steve Fanelli

Hook: TMC 5262, #12-#18
Thread: Black UNI 8/0
Tail: One black goose biot
Body: Black Hareline rabbit dubbing
Spines: Black goose biots, 4-5 depending upon fly size

Top view

Comments: Steve Fanelli notes, "This fly has been an exceptional exploring pattern. I usually fish it dead drift with an occasional twitch."

Superior X Legs

Pattern type: General attractor, stonefly nymph
Submitted by: The Superior Fly Angler (Superior, Wisconsin)
Originated by: Jim Pollock
Tied by: Jim Pollock

Hook: Mustad 9671, #10-#12
Thread: Brown
Tail: Brown marabou
Body: Kaufmann Brown Stone dubbing; thorax tied with dubbing loop
Ribbing: Medium copper wire,
Legs: Brown Sili-legs

Top view

TP's Beadhead Pheasant Ear Purple

Pattern type: General attractor, stonefly nymph
Submitted by: The Sporting Gentleman of Delaware (Centreville, Delaware)
Originated by: Terry Peach
Tied by: Terry Peach

Hook: Nymph 2XL, #12
Thread: Purple 6/0
Tail: Purple pheasant tail fibers
Abdomen: Purple rabbit/Antron blend dubbing
Ribbing: Copper wire, counterwrapped
Wing case: Purple pheasant tail fibers
Thorax: Purple/black rabbit/Antron blend dubbing
Legs: Purple pheasant tail fibers
Head: 1/8" brass bead

Top view

Tunghead Lite Brite Prince Nymph

Top view

Pattern type:	General attractor
Submitted by:	Bob Mitchell's Fly Shop (Lake Elmo, Minnesota)
Originated by:	Michael Alwin
Tied by:	Murry Humble
Hook:	TMC 5262, #12-#14
Thread:	Black 6/0
Tail:	Reddish-brown goose biots
Body:	Peacock Lite Brite, cut to 1" lengths, dubbed and picked out
Ribbing:	Fine gold wire
Wings:	White goose biots
Hackle:	Brown, tied beard style
Head:	Brass-colored 1/8" tungsten bead underwrapped with lead wire

Comments: Fish this pattern deep or in off-color water with an upstream, dead drift.

Wet Flies

Carey Special (Variation)

Pattern type:	General attractor
Submitted by:	The Superior Fly Angler (Superior, Wisconsin)
Originated by:	Colonel Carey
Tied by:	Matt Paulson
Hook:	Mustad 9672, #4-#8
Thread:	Black 6/0
Tail:	Pheasant rump feather fibers
Body:	Peacock herl
Ribbing:	Fine copper wire, counterwrapped
Hackle:	Pheasant rump feather

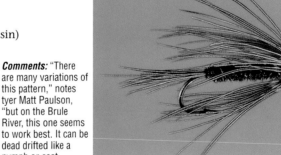

Comments: "There are many variations of this pattern," notes tyer Matt Paulson, "but on the Brule River, this one seems to work best. It can be dead drifted like a nymph or cast across-and-down and then stripped back, like fishing a soft hackle."

Killer

Pattern type:	General attractor
Submitted by:	Whitetop Laurel Fly Shop (West Jefferson, North Carolina)
Originated by:	Lowell A. Shipe
Tied by:	Lowell A. Shipe
Hook:	Mustad 3906B, #14
Thread:	Yellow 6/0 prewaxed
Tail:	Lemon wood duck fibers
Body:	Herl from peacock eye twisted with copper wire and wrapped
Wing:	Lemon wood duck fibers
Hackle:	3 wraps of light ginger

Comments: This wet fly has proven itself on the streams of northwest North Carolina, southwest Virginia, and northeast Tennessee. To fish deep, apply lead to the leader rather than the fly body.

Pass Lake

Pattern type: General attractor
Submitted by: River's Edge Fly Shop (Thunder Bay, Ontario)
Originated by: unknown
Tied by: Doug Melville

Hook: Mustad 3906, #14
Thread: Black 8/0
Tail: Brown hackle fibers
Body: Black wool, single strand from 4-ply yarn
Wing: White calf tail topped with 2-4 strands pearl Krystal Flash
Hackle: Brown Indian rooster

Comments: The Krystal Flash topping on the wing is optional, but recommended.

Pass Lake

Pattern type: General attractor
Submitted by: The Superior Fly Angler (Superior, Wisconsin)
Originated by: unknown
Tied by: Matt Paulson

Hook: Mustad 9671, #8-#12
Thread: Black 6/0
Tail: Brown hackle fibers
Body: Black chenille, medium
Wing: White calf tail
Hackle: Brown hen

Comments: Matt Paulson fishes this fly against cedar-shaded banks of the upper Brule River in Wisconsin.

Pass Lake (Variation)

Pattern type: General attractor
Submitted by: The Superior Fly Angler (Superior, Wisconsin)
Originated by: Keith Behn adaptation of original pattern
Tied by: Keith Behn

Hook: TMC 5263BL, #8-#12; weighted with 12 wraps .020" or.025" lead wire
Thread: Black UNI 8/0
Tail: Brown hackle fibers
Body: Peacock Super Bright dubbing
Ribbing: Gold wire
Wing: White calf tail
Hackle: Soft, brown hen hackle

Tandy's Spider

Comments: To dress the pattern, tie in body feather so that the tip forms a tail. At the butt of the feather, stroke a few fibers outward to form the hackle later. Wrap the feather to form the body, then continue wrapping so that the fibers at the butts form a collar hackle. Dan Rivard advises fishing this pattern deep—using a 2- to 4-foot section of lead-core line at the tip of the fly line and a 3- to 5-foot leader.

Pattern type: General attractor
Submitted by: Dan's Fly Shop (Roscommon, Michigan)
Originated by: Dan Rivard and Tandy Ferguson
Tied by: Dan Rivard

Hook: Wet fly, #6-#16; or 3XL to 4XL, #6-#12
Thread: Flat 3/0 to match body color
Tail: Tip of feather used for body
Body: Flank feather from mallard hen or drake, crow, pheasant, or other bird
Ribbing (opt.): Silver or copper wire
Hackle: Butt fibers of body feather

West Branch Special

Pattern type: General attractor
Submitted by: Theriault Flies (Patten, Maine)
Originated by: unknown
Tied by: Alvin Theriault

Hook: Mustad 9761, #8
Thread: Black 6/0 prewaxed
Body: Bright orange yarn
Wings: White domestic goat hair
Hackle: Red calf tail

Comments: This wet fly was designed for brook trout in the ponds of Baxter State Park and waters in the West Branch area.

Streamers

Alexandria

Pattern type: General attractor
Submitted by: Great Lakes Outfitters (Tonawanda, New York)
Originated by: W.G. Turle
Tied by: Michael Donohue

Hook: Mustad 9672, #6-#10
Thread: Black
Tail: Red grizzly hackle fibers
Body: Flat silver tinsel
Ribbing: Oval silver tinsel
Wings: Red grizzly hackle tips topped with peacock sword herl
Hackle: Black

Comments: Tyer Michael Donohue says, "I have adapted this pattern from the original by the use of red grizzly hackle instead of red goose quill because I have found that it's more streamlined in the water and spooks fewer trout, especially heavily fished ones. It's best as a cold-water pattern."

Algonquin Streamer

Pattern type: General attractor
Submitted by: Quest Outdoors Orvis Fly Fishing Shop (Louisville, Kentucky)
Originated by: Norman Wathen
Tied by: Norman Wathen

Hook: Daiichi 2370, #2
Thread: Black size A Monocord
Body: Orange silk floss
Butt and ribbing: Flat silver tinsel
Belly: 4-5 peacock herls over sparse white bucktail
Wings: 2 black saddle hackles flanked by 2 red/orange saddle hackles flanked by 2 silver doctor blue saddle hackles
Shoulder: Mallard flank
Eyes: Jungle cock
Throat: Silver doctor blue hackle fibers

Comments: This attractor/smelt pattern is designed primarily for landlocked salmon.

Battenkill Lady Amherst

Pattern type: General attractor, moth
Submitted by: Gloria Jordan's Fly Rod Shop (Manchester Center, Vermont)
Originated by: Gloria Jordan
Tied by: Gloria Jordan

Hook: Mustad 9575, #10
Thread: Black
Tail: Golden pheasant crest
Body: Peacock herl
Ribbing: Fine gold tinsel
Wing: Lady Amherst red crest over Lady Amherst cape feathers flanked by golden pheasant tippet
Throat: Peacock sword

Comments: Gloria Jordan notes, "This fly was designed for the Battenkill and Mettawee rivers. It's a great fly to fish the riffles and a good attractor to fish any time of the day—especially toward dusk when big browns are feeding. Cast the streamer a bit upriver and across, stripping and mending any slack line. Twitch the tip of the rod slightly to give the fly a swimming movement. Always follow through on the cast, for many times just as the line straightens out, a trout will hit."

Ben's Blue Shiner

Pattern type: General attractor, baitfish
Submitted by: Backcast Fly Shop (Benzonia, Michigan)
Originated by: Ben Forrester
Tied by: Ben Forrester

Hook: Mustad 9672 or 36890, #6-#8
Thread: Black
Tail: Red calf tail
Body: Pearlescent pearl tinsel chenille
Wing: Blue calf tail over gray calf tail
Throat: Red calf tail

Comments: This baitfish/attractor fly incorporates red material to suggest a wounded minnow.

B.T. Matuka Shiner

Pattern type: General attractor, baitfish
Submitted by: Quest Outdoors Orvis Fly Fishing Shop (Louisville, Kentucky)
Originated by: Norman Wathen
Tied by: Norman Wathen

Hook: Daiichi J141 Bob Johns, #2
Thread: Yellow size A Monocord
Weed guard (opt.): Monofilament loop
Butt: Black tying thread, lacquered
Tail: White Craft Fur
Body: Gold Poly Flash
Wing: Tied in 4 separate bunches alternating with wraps of body material. From rear of hook, first 3 bunches are yellow Craft Fur topped with gold Krystal Flash; last bunch is rust Craft Fur
Throat: Red Krystal Flash over mixed colors of Krystal Flash
Head: Tying thread colored rust on top with permanent marker
Eyes: Painted, cream with rust pupil

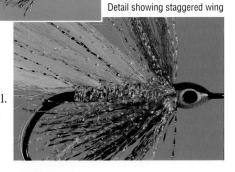

Detail showing staggered wing

Cactus Fly

Pattern type: General attractor
Submitted by: River's Edge Fly Shop (Thunder Bay, Ontario)
Originated by: Scott E. Smith and Mike Sewards
Tied by: Scott E. Smith

Hook: TMC 105 or Daiichi 2571, #4-#10`
Thread: Red UNI 6/0
Tail: Philoplume (aftershaft) dyed orange (pink for pink version)
Body: Pearl Cactus Chenille (pink for pink version)
Wing: Philoplume (aftershaft) dyed orange (pink for pink version)

Pink version

Comments: This pattern can be dressed in a variety of color combinations.

Chartreuse Sword

Pattern type: General attractor
Submitted by: The Sporting Gentleman (Media, Pennsylvania)
Originated by: Jim McAndrew
Tied by: Jim McAndrew

Hook: 6XL streamer, #6
Thread: Chartreuse for underbody, black for head
Body: Chartreuse floss
Ribbing: Flat silver embossed tinsel
Wings: 2 chartreuse schlappen feathers
Throat: Peacock sword herl
Head: Black tying thread

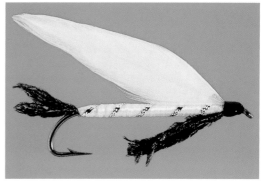

Comments: This pattern fishes well on newly stocked trout early in the season.

Cowen's Spinner Bugger

Pattern type: General attractor
Submitted by: The Fish Hawk (Atlanta, Georgia)
Originated by: Henry Cowen
Tied by: Henry Cowen

Hook: Mustad 79580 or 4XL streamer hook, #4-#12
Thread: Black UNI 8/0 (olive for olive/black version)
Trailer: Gold or silver Colorado spinner blade mounted on loop of 30lb mono
Tail: Black marabou (olive for olive/black version) and pearl Flashabou
Body: Black/orange variegated chenille (olive/black variegated for olive/black version)
Hackle: Brown (grizzly for olive/black version)
Head: Gold or silver bead

Olive/black version

Comments: This fly was originally tied for Connecticut's Housatonic River but has proven effective in Georgia's Chattahoochee River and other waters. Henry Cowen says, "It is the best searching pattern I have ever fished for trout in both rivers and lakes. Indiana-style or willow leaf spinner blades can also be used."

Delaware River Muddler

Pattern type: General attractor
Submitted by: Delaware River Anglers (Willow Grove, Pennsylvania)
Originated by: Ken Schwam version of Don Gapen design
Tied by: Ken Schwam

Hook: Mustad 36620, #6-#8; weighted with .025" lead wire
Thread: Tan UNI 6/0
Tail: Mottled turkey quill
Body: Gold tinsel chenille
Wings: Lynx hair (or other soft, mottled tan hair) between mottled turkey quill segments
Collar: Hair tips from head
Head: Spun deer hair, sparse

Comments: This fly resembles a variety of prey species found in a trout stream. It works equally well on warmwater fish.

Duzzie

Pattern type: General ttractor
Submitted by: Perry's Trout Fly Shop (Duluth, Minnesota)
Originated by: Elmer Wallin
Tied by: Perry A. Rowlison

Hook: Mustad 9672, #4-#10
Thread: Black 3/0 Monocord
Tail: Red calf tail
Body: Orange yarn
Ribbing: Embossed silver tinsel, counterwrapped
Wings: Gray squirrel tail
Hackle: Brown

Comments: The stillwater streamer was designed for lake fishing in the Boundary Waters Area of northern Minnesota.

Gary's Alien

Pattern type: General attractor
Submitted by: Gary's Flies (Mertztown, Pennsylvania)
Originated by: Gary Selig
Tied by: Gary Selig

Hook: Daiichi 2220, #6
Thread: Black UNI 8/0
Tail: 5 strands pearl Krystal Flash flanked by one small bunch chartreuse arctic fox or Finn raccoon (from Bow Tyer) on each side
Underbody: Wool, wrapped to shape
Body: Black pearl squirrel dubbing brush (from Enrico Puglisi, Ltd.)
Hackle: Grade #1 Metz furnace saddle
Head: 3/16" Spirit River chartreuse Hot Bead

Golden Squirrel

Pattern type: General attractor
Submitted by: River's Edge Fly Shop (Thunder Bay, Ontario)
Originated by: Royce Damm
Tied by: Doug Melville

Hook: Mustad 98431, #10
Thread: Black 6/0
Tail (opt.): Red hackle fibers
Body: Flat gold tinsel
Throat: Red hackle fibers, sparse
Wing: Red pine squirrel tail, sparse
Cheeks (opt.): Small jungle cock eyes, tied in short

Green-butt Monkey

Pattern type: General attractor
Submitted by: River's Edge Fly Shop (Thunder Bay, Ontario)
Originated by: Scott E. Smith and Bob Linsenman
Tied by: Scott E. Smith

Hook: TMC 300 or Daiichi 2220, #2-#4; weighted with lead wire
Thread: 6/0 UNI
Tail: Chartreuse marabou with several strands gold Krystal Flash
Body: Gold tinsel chenille
Ribbing: Gold wire
Wing: Rusty brown rabbit strip, tied Matuka style
Throat: Red yarn
Hackle: Pheasant rump dyed rusty brown
Head: Tan ram's wool

Comments: To form the head on this pattern, tie 4-6 cigar-sized clumps of wool tightly to the shank. Tease up the wool fibers with a dubbing needle, and clip the head to shape. The tan wool, by the way, is produced by dyeing white wool in strong, black coffee.

Hare's Ear Woolly Bugger

Pattern type: General attractor
Submitted by: Fly Angler (Fridley, Minnesota)
Originated by: Chris Hansen
Tied by: Chris Hansen

Hook: 3XL nymph, #4-#12
Thread: Red 6/0
Tail: Coyote fur with some guard hairs left in
Body: Light sowbug Wapsi Sow Scud dubbing
Hackle: Barred ginger or cree saddle
Ribbing: Gold wire

Comments: "This fly," explains Chris Hansen, "works well in a variety of situations. A long upstream cast with a fast retrieve works well on flats; a dead drift is effective in deep runs; or fish it down-and-across in larger streams. Depending on how you fish it, the fly can pass for a baitfish, crayfish, or a hex nymph."

Jim's Gem

Pattern type: General attractor
Submitted by: Chesapeake Fly & Bait Company (Arnold, Maryland)
Originated by: Jim Hester
Tied by: Jim Hester

Hook: Mustad 9671 or Mustad 9672, #6-#10; weighted with several wraps of fine lead wire
Thread: Black or chartreuse Danville Flymaster 6/0
Tail: Black marabou
Abdomen: Pearlescent black Micro Cactus Chenille
Thorax: Pearlescent chartreuse Cactus Chenille

Comments: This is a favorite searching pattern.

Jonathan's Fury (Chartreuse)

Pattern type: General attractor
Submitted by: Eldredge Bros. Fly Shop (Cape Neddick, Maine)
Originated by: Kent Bartley
Tied by: Kent Bartley

Hook: Mustad 94720 or Partridge CS15, #2/0-#4
Thread: Chartreuse 6/0
Tail: Chartreuse hackle fibers
Body: Clear or pearlescent tubing
Belly: White Super Hair over chartreuse bucktail
Throat: Red rabbit fur
Wings: Peacock herl over chartreuse Krystal Flash over chartreuse bucktail, flanked by 1 chartreuse saddle hackle on each side
Eyes: 4.5mm gold plastic

Jonathan's Fury (Orange)

Pattern type: General attractor
Submitted by: Eldredge Bros. Fly Shop (Cape Neddick, Maine)
Originated by: Kent Bartley
Tied by: Kent Bartley

Hook: Mustad 94720 or Partridge CS15, #2/0-#10
Thread: Fire orange UNI 6/0
Tail: Orange hackle fibers
Body: Gold tubing
Belly: White Super Hair over orange bucktail
Throat: Red rabbit fur
Wings: Peacock herl over orange bucktail flanked by 1 orange saddle hackle on each side
Eyes: 4.5mm gold plastic

Ken's Copperhead

Pattern type: General attractor
Submitted by: Nestor's Sporting Goods, Inc. (Quakertown and Whitehall, Pennsylvania)
Originated by: Kenneth W. Mead
Tied by: Kenneth W. Mead

Hook: Streamer 3XL-4XL, #2-#14
Thread: Red Danville 6/0
Tail: Root beer marabou
Body: Peacock herl
Ribbing: Medium copper wire
Hackle: Furnace, palmered over body
Gills: Band of red tying thread
Head: Copper bead (5/32" for hooks #6-#12)

Comments: Tyer Ken Mead sometimes dresses this pattern with a yellow under-tail.

Last Day

Pattern type: General attractor
Submitted by: Thom's of Maine (Houlton, Maine)
Originated by: Thom Willard
Tied by: Thom Willard

Hook: Front—Mustad 3906B #4; Rear—Mustad 3906 #6
Thread: Black UNI 6/0
Tail: Golden pheasant crest
Body: Orange UNI-Stretch
Ribbing: Embossed silver tinsel
Wings: 2 bright red and 2 orange grizzly saddle hackles topped with 3 strands peacock herl
Throat: Yellow polar bear
Eyes: Painted yellow with black pupils

Comments: This is an excellent trolling fly at ice-out as well as in the late season—hence the name, Last Day. It can also be tied on a single long-shank hook and cast for trout and land-locked salmon.

Lester Brown

Pattern type: General attractor
Submitted by: Superior Fly Angler (Superior, Wisconsin)
Originated by: Larry Markley
Tied by: Larry Markley

Hook: Mustad 36890, #8
Thread: Brown Kevlar
Tail: Brown marabou
Body: Brown chenille
Wing: Brown marabou

Matt's Brat

Pattern type: General attractor
Submitted by: Thom's of Maine (Houlton, Maine)
Originated by: Thom Willard
Tied by: Thom Willard

Hook: Tandem version, Front—Mustad 3906B, #6; Rear—Mustad 3906, #6; joined by nylon-coated stranded steel wire. Single-hook version, 8XL streamer
Thread: Black UNI 6/0
Body: Fuchsia UNI-Stretch nylon, lacquered
Ribbing: Fine embossed silver metal tinsel
Throat: Polar bear dyed salmon-egg
Wings: 6 strands purple Krystal Flash over 2 light blue saddle hackles, flanked by 2 cree hackles dyed gray
Cheeks: Silver pheasant feathers, tied above shank
Eyes: Painted, yellow with red pupils

Micro Bugger

Chartreuse version

Pattern type: General attractor
Submitted by: Chesapeake Fly & Bait Company (Arnold, Maryland)
Originated by: Jim Hester
Tied by: Jim Hester

Hook: Mustad 9672, #6-#12; weight optional
Thread: Fluorescent red or black Danville Flymaster 6/0
Tail: Black marabou (chartreuse for chartreuse version)
Body: Black chenille (chartreuse for chartreuse version), medium or small
Ribbing: Pearlescent Micro Cactus Chenille

Comments: Jim Hester ties this pattern in white, brown, and olive as well. He uses red thread for weighted flies and black thread for unweighted ones in order to tell them apart easily in his fly box.

Papa's Poacher

Pattern type: General attractor
Submitted by: Thom's of Maine (Houlton, Maine)
Originated by: Thom Willard
Tied by: Thom Willard

Hook: Front—Mustad 3906B, #6; Rear—Mustad 3906, #6; connected with nylon-coated stranded steel wire
Thread: Black UNI 6/0
Body: Chartreuse UNI-Stretch nylon, front and rear hooks
Ribbing: Gold Mylar tinsel, front and rear hooks
Throat: Orange/yellow calf tail
Wings: 9 strands yellow Krystal Flash, flanked by 1 hot orange saddle hackle per side, flanked by 1 bright yellow saddle hackle per side
Cheeks: Mallard flank dyed dark purple
Eyes: Painted, red with yellow pupils

Peacock Bugger

Pattern type: General attractor
Submitted by: The Superior Fly Angler (Superior, Wisconsin)
Originated by: unknown
Tied by: Keith Behn

Hook: TMC 7999, #4-#10
Thread: Black 3/0 for larger hooks, black 8/0 for smaller sizes
Tail: Black marabou
Body: Peacock herl
Hackle: Black saddle hackled, palmered
Ribbing: Copper wire

Comments: This fly can be weighted with lead wire for faster or deeper water.

Pink Lady

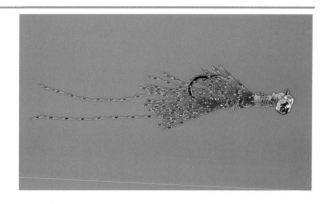

Pattern type: General attractor
Submitted by: The Bear's Den Fly Fishing Shoppe (Taunton, Massachusetts)
Originated by: Thomas Martin
Tied by: Thomas Martin

Hook: 3XL, #14
Thread: White
Throat: Pink Krystal Flash
Belly: Pink Krystal Flash
Eyes: Silver bead chain

Rag-A-Muddler

Pattern type: General attractor, baitfish
Submitted by: Riverbend Sport Shop (Southfield, Michigan)
Originated by: Brian Hanchin
Tied by: Brian Hanchin

Hook: 3XL streamer, #2-#12
Thread: Tan UNI 6/0
Tail: Light fibers from chukar partridge body feather
Body: Copper wire (lacquering optional)
Wing: A few strands tan Krystal Flash over gray squirrel tail
Throat: Tan or red Krystal Flash or marabou
Collar: Dark gray fluff from base of pheasant, grouse, or other game bird feather, spun in dubbing loop

Comments: The collar on this pattern should be dressed thickly, not tightly spun and dubbed. These natural fibers pulsate wildly when the fly is retrieved.

Red Eyed Bugger

Pattern type: General attractor
Submitted by: Dakota Angler & Outfitter (Rapid City, South Dakota)
Originated by: Jim Smoragiewicz variation of Woolly Bugger
Tied by: Jim Smoragiewicz

Hook: TMC 5262 or Daiichi 1710, #8-#12
Thread: Olive Benecchi 8/0
Tail: Olive (or black) marabou
Body: Peacock Kreinik Micro Ice Chenille
Hackle: Olive saddle hackle
Collar: Red dubbing
Head: Gold metal bead

Rivergod Bugger

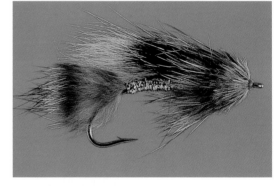

Pattern type: General attractor
Submitted by: Great Lakes Fly Fishing Company (Rockford, Michigan)
Originated by: Dennis M. Potter
Tied by: Dennis M. Potter

Hook: TMC 9395, #4-#8; rear half of shank weighted
Thread: Black 3/0
Tail: Black marabou blood feathers
Body: Peacock herl
Lateral line: 3-4 strands of Crystal Hair, held in place with hackle and left long for tail
Hackle: Black dry-fly quality

Comments: Dennis Potter explains, "I normally weight only the back half of the hook. When the fly is fished with a short strip-pause, it falls butt-first on the pause, creating a wonderful action with the tail and collar. The dry-fly hackle may produce more noise in the water than long, soft saddle hackle." To dress the hackle, space the last 3-5 wraps so that the fluffy, marabou-like butt of the feather is wrapped as a collar behind the hook eye.

Road Kill Muddler

Pattern type: General attractor
Submitted by: Fly and Field (Glen Ellyn, Illinois)
Originated by: Bob Dulian
Tied by: Bob Dulian

Hook: TMC 200, #4-#10
Thread: Gray Danville 6/0
Tail: Cottontail rabbit fur
Body: Gold braid
Wing: Gray squirrel tail
Collar: Rabbit fur spun in dubbing loop
Head: Rabbit fur with guard hairs removed, spun in dubbing loop

Shenk's Pearly Killer

Below: Version with Stick-On Eyes
The feather on the near side is lifted to show the Fishair and Krystal Flash underwing.

Pattern type: General attractor, baitfish
Submitted by: South Mountain Custom Rod & Tackle (Lebanon, Pennsylvania)
Originated by: David R. Shenk
Tied by: David R. Shenk

Hook: Mustad 3665A or TMC 300, #6-#14
Thread: Black
Tail: Black FisHair
Body: White Sparkle Antron
Wing: Pearlescent Krystal Flash over black FisHair flanked by one mallard breast feather per side
Head: Fine lead wire overwrapped with white rod-winding thread, covered with 3 coats white vinyl jig enamel
Eyes (opt.): Stick-On Eyes coated with 5-minute epoxy

Comments: David Shenk notes that this fly has proven effective all over the United States, not only for trout, but for large-mouth and smallmouth bass, lake trout, and even striped bass. Fish it with a strip retrieve that makes the fly dart.

Strip Leech (Black)

Pattern type: General attractor
Submitted by: River's Edge Fly Shop (Thunder Bay, Ontario)
Originated by: Bill Boote version of Gary Borger design
Tied by: Romeo Rancourt

Hook: Daiichi 2220, #2-#8; weighted full length with lead wire of same diameter as hook shank
Thread: Black 3/0 Monocord
Tail: Black marabou flanked with 4 strands pearl Krystal Flash on each side
Body: Black Crystal Chenille
Ribbing: #27 French silver wire, counterwrapped
Wing: Black rabbit strip, tied Matuka style
Hackle: Pheasant rump dyed black

Comments: The series of Strip Leech flies that follow were designed primarily for fishing Ontario's Nipigon River and the big brook trout there. Originator Bill Boote ranks this fly design right up with the Woolly Bugger and Muddler for taking big trout consistently. This black version works best in clear water and is responsible for a brook trout of better than 9 pounds on the Nipigon.

Strip Leech (Natural)

Pattern type: General attractor
Submitted by: River's Edge Fly Shop (Thunder Bay, Ontario)
Originated by: Bill Boote version of Gary Borger design
Tied by: Romeo Rancourt

Hook: Daiichi 2220, #2-#8; weighted full length with lead wire of same diameter as hook shank
Thread: Brown 3/0 Monocord
Tail: Chartreuse marabou flanked with 4 strands chartreuse Krystal Flash on each side
Body: Gold tinsel chenille
Ribbing: #27 French brass wire
Wing: Natural brown rabbit strip, tied Matuka style
Hackle: Pheasant rump

Strip Leech (Olive)

Pattern type: General attractor
Submitted by: River's Edge Fly Shop (Thunder Bay, Ontario)
Originated by: Bill Boote version of Gary Borger design
Tied by: Romeo Rancourt

Hook: Daiichi 2220, #2-#8; weighted full length with lead wire of same diameter as hook shank
Thread: Olive 3/0 Monocord
Tail: Chartreuse marabou flanked with 4 strands chartreuse Krystal Flash on each side
Body: Olive Mohair
Ribbing: #27 French silver wire, counterwrapped
Wing: Chinchilla rabbit strip dyed olive, tied Matuka style
Hackle: Pheasant rump dyed olive

Comments: Of the Strip Leech series from the River's Edge Fly Shop, this particular pattern is Bill Boote's favorite. It's excellent in off-colored water.

Strip Leech (Orange)

Pattern type: General attractor
Submitted by: River's Edge Fly Shop (Thunder Bay, Ontario)
Originated by: Bill Boote version of Gary Borger design
Tied by: Romeo Rancourt

Hook: Daiichi 2220, #2-#8; weighted full length with lead wire of same diameter as hook shank
Thread: Black 3/0 Monocord
Tail: Chartreuse marabou flanked with 4 strands chartreuse Krystal Flash on each side
Body: Gold tinsel chenille
Ribbing: #27 French brass wire, counterwrapped
Wing: Chinchilla rabbit strip dyed orange, tied Matuka style
Hackle: Pheasant rump dyed orange

Comments: This fall pattern is particularly effective for coaster brook trout.

Strip Leech (Silver)

Pattern type: General attractor
Submitted by: River's Edge Fly Shop (Thunder Bay, Ontario)
Originated by: Bill Boote version of Gary Borger design
Tied by: Romeo Rancourt

Hook: Daiichi 2220, #2-#8; weighted full length with lead wire of same diameter as hook shank
Thread: Red 3/0 Monocord
Tail: White marabou flanked with 4 strands pearl Krystal Flash on each side
Body: Silver tinsel chenille
Ribbing: #27 French silver wire
Wing: White rabbit strip, tied Matuka style
Throat: Red marabou
Hackle: Silver pheasant body feather

Super Weasel

Pattern type: Baitfish and general attractor
Submitted by: Flies for Michigan (N. Muskegon, Michigan)
Originated by: Al Rockwood
Tied by: Al Rockwood

Hook: Mustad 9672, #6-#10
Thread: Red size A twisted nylon
Body: .035" non-toxic wire on front half of shank, overwrapped with blue silk thread
Wings: 3 mallard flank feathers
Collar: Pearl Krystal Flash
Head: Red thread coated with 5-minute epoxy

Comments: This pattern, notes Al Rockwood, "should be stripped vigorously to imitate an Injured minnow. It works in both lakes and streams. I find it most effective when the water is slightly dirty, or in the spring and fall when insects are less available."

Utter Chaos

Pattern type: General attractor
Submitted by: Sodie's (St. George, Kansas)
Originated by: Craig Phillips version of Paul Sodamann's Cattail Leech
Tied by: Craig Phillips

Hook: Mustad 9672, #10-#16; weighted with lead wire along entire shank
Thread: Tan or black UNI 6/0
Tail: Dark hair from underside of cat tail
Body: Body hair combed from Shar-pai dog

Comments: "This fly," says tyer Craig Phillips, "is my variation of Paul Sodamann's very successful Cattail Leech pattern (see p. 112). While Sodie used prepared dubbing for most of his leeches, I use the short, stiff hairs from a Shar-pai, spun in a dubbing loop. The name derives from a line Bill Murray spoke in a movie, 'dogs and cats, living together, utter chaos.' This fly has produced trout in the White River of Arkansas when fished deep with a very slow retrieve. It is also a very effective warmwater pattern."

White Collar Bugger

Top view

Pattern type: General attractor
Submitted by: The Forks Fly Shop (Inglewood, Ontario)
Originated by: Wayne F. Martin
Tied by: Wayne F. Martin

Hook: Partridge H3ST Draper, #14-#16; weighted (see Comments)
Thread: Black
Tail: Black marabou
Body: Rear 3/4, black rabbit dubbing; front 1/4, red floss
Hackle: Black saddle
Wings: White goose biots

Comments: Although developed for rainbows in the Great Lakes, this fly produces on rivers and stillwaters almost everywhere. The Draper hook used has a double shank and can be weighted in one of two ways. The weight can be tied between the double shanks, or the shanks can be wrapped with thread and the weight laid atop the thread-wrapped double-shank, in which case the fly will ride point-up to prevent most bottom snags. The hackle is mounted by the tip at the rear of the hook and wrapped forward. The fuzzy base of the feather should end up wrapped behind the hook eye.

Eggs

Chenille Skein

Pattern type: Drifting eggs
Submitted by: Orleans Outdoor (Albion, New York)
Originated by: Mike Prairie
Tied by: Mike Prairie

Hook: Daiichi 1530 or equivalent, #8-#14
Thread: Pink or orange pre-waxed 6/0
Body: Orange and cream chenille, twisted together

Top view

Bottom view

Comments: Shop owner Ron Bierstine explains, "Unlike most egg patterns, the Chenille Skein is tied to imitate a whole piece of skein. The two strands of chenille are twisted together and tied off in clumps to resemble an irregular assemblage of eggs. Don't let its simple bulk convince you that it won't be a productive fly. Because of its irregular shape, it has a unique tumbling action on a dead drift that browns and rainbows can't resist." The fly is also tied in chartreuse/orange and orange/cerise.

Mark's Carpet Fly

Pattern type: Drifting eggs
Submitted by: Orleans Outdoor (Albion, New York)
Originated by: Mark Stothard
Tied by: Mark Stothard

Hook: Daiichi 1530, #10-#14
Thread: Orange Kevlar
Body: Standard knitting yarn, mix of white, orange, cadmium yellow, yellow ochre, pink, peach, light yellow

Comments: First tied for salmon and migratory trout, this fly works on stream trout as well. Shop owner Ron Bierstine notes, "The pattern is tied like a Glo-Bug, but incorporates many colors that may make the fly look like a small cluster of eggs. The fly is typically tied with 7 strands of yarn for a #10 hook, 6 strands for a #12, and 10 half-strands for #14. The yarn is positioned toward the eye of the hook to leave the gap open."

Scrambled Eggs

Pattern type: Drifting eggs
Submitted by: Orleans Outdoor (Albion, New York)
Originated by: John Miller
Tied by: John Miller

Hook: Mustad 3906, #10-#14
Thread: Chartreuse Danville flat waxed nylon or 3/0 (or color to match body)
Body: Chartreuse Glo-Bug Yarn

Bottom view

Comments: Shop owner Ron Bierstine explains, "Scrambled Eggs was originally designed for migratory trout and salmon, but it works equally well for inland stream trout that may be feeding on trout eggs. The Glo-Bug Yarn is clumped atop the shank and split with the tying thread in order to resemble a small cluster of eggs. The size of the clump of yarn depends on hook size. The yarn is clipped short at the head and tail of the fly to approximate an egg at either end." Bierstine notes that the pattern is effective in other colors as well: pink lady, Oregon cheese, and orange.

CHAPTER 2

Mayflies

Nymphs

Baetis, Master

Pattern type: *Baetis* nymph
Submitted by: The Fish Hawk (Atlanta, Georgia)
Originated by: Robert Rooks, Jr.
Tied by: Robert Rooks, Jr.

Hook: Partridge Oliver Edwards K14ST, #16-#20
Thread: Olive dun UNI 8/0
Tail: Bronze mallard fibers
Abdomen: Olive dun UNI 8/0, built up
Ribbing: Chartreuse UNI 3/0, twisted tightly and counterwrapped
Wing case: Turkey tail segment
Thorax: SLF Hatch Match HM7 brown/olive dubbing
Legs: Barred gadwall flank fibers

Comments: Robert Rooks notes that this is the best BWO nymph pattern that he's fished. It can also be tied with a small black nickel bead head.

Baetis Nymph

Pattern type: *Baetis* nymph
Submitted by: Adventure Fly Fishing (Greensboro, North Carolina)
Originated by: Jeff Wilkins
Tied by: Jeff Wilkins

Hook: TMC 3769 or TMC 100, #18-#24
Thread: Black UNI 8/0
Tail: Black hackle fibers
Body: Black Superfine dubbing
Ribbing: 5x tippet material
Wing case: Black hackle fibers from tail
Legs: Black hackle fibers from wing case, 3 per side

Top view

Comments: This nymph is dressed in a style devised by Andre Puyans. The black hackle fibers that form the tail and wingcase are mounted at mid-shank. The thread is wrapped back to the hook bend, and fibers are trimmed to leave the desired number remaining for the tail. The butt ends of the fiber form the wingcase, and finally, the legs. This style makes possible a slender, shiny wingcase. "This Baetis/BWO pattern," says Jeff Wilkins, "is an early season favorite."

Biot Baetis Nymph

Top view

Pattern type: *Baetis* nymph
Submitted by: Adventure Fly Fishing (Greensboro, North Carolina)
Originated by: Jeff Wilkins
Tied by: Jeff Wilkins

Hook: Orvis 1524, #18; or TMC 200R, #20-#22
Thread: Olive or black UNI 8/0
Tail: Dark dun Micro Fibbets
Abdomen: Black, dark brown, or olive turkey biot
Ribbing: Danville Monothread or 5x tippet material
Thorax: Black Umpqua/Paxton's Buggy Nymph dubbing
Legs: Black or very dark brown hen hackle
Wing case: Turkey biot, tied in behind hook eye, trimmed to "V" at rear

Comments: Jeff Wilkins notes, "This nymph is tied to match our early season *Baetis* hatches. Although usually tied in olive, we like to use a dark brown to black imitation which is a better match for the flies in our area. The turkey biot abdomen makes it possible to keep this portion of the body skinny, a trait very obvious in this type of nymph. An all-olive or grass green version does well with the late-season BWOs, or *Pseudocloeons*, and in this version, we tie the pattern without the legs."

Coleman's Hendrickson Nymph Oatka

Bottom view

Pattern type: Hendrickson nymph
Submitted by: Coleman's Fly Shop (Spencerport, New York)
Originated by: Carl Coleman
Tied by: Carl Coleman

Hook: Daiichi 1710, #12
Thread: Brown UNI 6/0
Tail: Pine squirrel tail
Abdomen: Mad River dubbing, 1 part #9, 1 part #18, 1 part #22
Ribbing: Fine gold oval tinsel
Wing case: Dark gray goose quill
Thorax: Hare's mask with guard hairs, loosely dubbed
Legs: Pine squirrel tail

Comments: The legs on this pattern are formed after the wing case has been mounted and the thorax dubbed. Tie in a clump of pine squirrel tail 1/8" in diameter on top of the shank ahead of the thorax. Draw the wing case forward, splitting the clump of squirrel hair into two equal bundles, positioned as in the photo. Trim the hair tips so that the legs are no longer than the body. Fish the fly across and down, with or without weight, below riffles and near stream banks. It can be retrieved slowly.

Crystal Pheasant Tail

Pattern type: Mayfly nymph
Submitted by: Choo Choo Fly & Tackle (Chattanooga, Tennessee)
Originated by: Ryan Meulemans
Tied by: Ryan Meulemans

Hook: TMC 3761, #12-#16
Thread: Tan 8/0
Tail: 5 pheasant tail fibers
Abdomen: 5 pheasant tail fibers
Ribbing: Fine copper wire
Thorax: Fox squirrel and olive Antron dubbing behind crystal bead
Hackle: Grizzly saddle

Dakota Nymph

Pattern type: Mayfly nymph
Submitted by: Dakota Angler & Outfitter (Rapid City, South Dakota)
Originated by: Jim Smoragiewicz
Tied by: Jim Smoragiewicz

Hook: Partridge GR7MMB (Jardine living nymph hook), #16
Thread: Brown Benecchi 10/0
Tail: Coyote leg fur
Body: Buffalo dubbing
Hackle: Sharptail grouse

Doc's Terminator

Pattern type: Hendrickson nymph
(*Ephemerella subvaria*)
Submitted by: Doc's Custom Tackle
(Portage, Michigan)
Originated by: Merrill S. Katz
Tied by: Merrill S. Katz

Hook: Partridge GRS4A, #10; or Mustad 9672,
#10-#14; weighted with a tapered
underbody formed from flat lead wire
Thread: Tobacco brown (Danville #47) 6/0 prewaxed
Tail: 3 pheasant tail fibers
Abdomen: Quill material stripped from shaft of mallard
primary feather
Ribbing: Fine copper wire counterwrapped over abdomen
Thorax: Peacock herl
Wing case: Quill segment from dark mallard
or goose primary feather
Legs: Partridge breast feather

Bottom view

Comments: This pattern was designed for streams in the "Grape Country" of southwestern Michigan and has produced well on the Pere Marquette, Big Manistee, Sturgeon, and Au Sable rivers. Merrill Katz often fishes this fly on the point, with a dropper above it, either dead-drifting upstream or quartering downstream. The legs are formed by tying the partridge feather at the rear of the thorax after mounting the wing case material. The thorax is tied, then the feather is drawn forward and tied off. The wing case is pulled over the partridge feather. The abdomen and ribbing are lacquered for durability.

E-Poxy Nymph

Pattern type: Mayfly nymph
Submitted by: The Fish Hawk (Atlanta, Georgia)
Originated by: Robert Rooks, Jr.
Tied by: Robert Rooks, Jr.

Hook: TMC 2302, #14-#18
Thread: Camel UNI 8/0
Tail: Pheasant tail fibers from shellback over
natural ostrich herl tips from gills
Abdomen: Dark gray mink dubbing
Gills: Natural ostrich herl palmered over abdomen
Shellback: Pheasant tail fibers
Ribbing: Gold wire, counterwrapped
Thorax: Peacock herl
Legs: Hungarian partridge saddle feather
Wing case: Drop of 5-minute epoxy on top of thorax

Bottom view

Comments: Abdomen color on this pattern can be changed to match a variety of naturals. The epoxy wing case is a Mike Mercer technique.

The EV Special

Pattern type: Mayfly nymph
Submitted by: Urban Angler Ltd. (New York, New York)
Originated by: Edwin Valentin
Tied by: Edwin Valentin

Hook: Mustad 94840, #14-#18
Thread: Olive or brown 6/0
Tail: Pheasant tail fibers
Abdomen: Olive beaver dubbing
Ribbing: Gold wire
Wing case: Turkey quill or pheasant tail fibers
Thorax: Olive ostrich herl
Head: Red thread

Comments: The EV Special is a nymph/emerger pattern for small streams like the East Branch of the Croton River.

Isonychia, Drifting

Top view

Pattern type: *Isonychia* nymph
Submitted by: The Fish Hawk (Atlanta, Georgia)
Originated by: Robert Rooks, Jr.
Tied by: Robert Rooks, Jr.

Hook: TMC 3761, #12-#14
Thread: Camel UNI 8/0
Tail: Pheasant tail fibers
Dorsal stripe: White moose mane fiber or stripped white hackle quill
Abdomen: Honey Nature's Spirit Dubbing
Ribbing: Small copper wire, counterwrapped
Thorax: Ephemerella SLF brown dubbing
Legs: Speckled hen hackle

Comments: This is an excellent pattern for fishing an *Isonychia* hatch, but is a good all-around attractor nymph as well.

Jay's Olive Pheasant Tail

Top view

Pattern type: Blue-winged olive nymph
Submitted by: Coleman's Fly Shop (Spencerport, New York)
Originated by: Jay Peck
Tied by: Jay Peck

Hook: Daiichi 1130, #16
Thread: Olive UNI 8/0
Tail: Olive pheasant tail fibers from abdomen
Abdomen: 3-4 olive pheasant tail fibers, twisted and wrapped
Ribbing: Fine copper wire, counterwrapped
Wing case: Olive pheasant tail fibers
Thorax: Fine peacock herl
Head: Small silver-lined gold glass bead (Umpqua)

Landis Leggo

Bottom view

Pattern type: *Ephemerella* (sulphur) nymph
Submitted by: Mountain Sports, Ltd. (Bristol, Virginia)
Originated by: Tim Landis
Tied by: Tim Landis

Hook: Daiichi 1550, Orvis 167T, or TMC 3769, #12-#16; weighted over thorax with .014" non-toxic wire
Thread: Tan 8/0
Tail: Wood duck flank fibers
Body: Light olive Antron Hare
Ribbing: Fine gold wire
Shellback: 7 pheasant tail fibers
Wing case: Pheasant tail fibers from shellback
Legs: Crimped pheasant tail fibers from wing case

Comments: This pattern was designed after tyer Tim Landis spent time observing sulphur nymphs on the South Holston River. He discovered that when the swimming nymphs pause, they freeze into a "hard-arch" posture with outstretched legs—the silhouette reproduced in this fly pattern. He has fished this fly successfully over much of North America.

In this pattern, the shellback, triple wing case, and legs are formed from the same pheasant tail fibers. Tie these fibers at the base of the tail, dub body, form shellback on abdomen, and rib with gold wire. After dubbing thorax, pull pheasant tail fibers toward hook eye and bind down as a conventional wing case. Bring tying thread under thorax to rear of wing case; pull pheasant tail fibers back over first wing case, and bind down to form a second wing case over the first. Bring tying under thorax to front of wing case; pull pheasant tail fibers forward; bind down over the tops of the fibers on previous 2 wing cases, not directly over the shank itself.

To form legs, pull 3 fibers to each side of hook; trim away the remaining fiber. Angle-cut the legs to length. With left thumb and forefinger, push trimmed legs fibers perpendicular to the shank; the fibers will cup forward. Pinch the leg fibers against the shank to crimp and create leg joints. Arrange legs with dubbing needle. Darken the top of the head with a waterproof marker. Place heavy drop of penetrating cement on thorax and head. Thoroughly coat legs with cement and arrange into final positions.

Latex Wiggler (Betsie Bug)

Pattern type: *Hexagenia* mayfly nymph
Submitted by: Backcast Fly Shop (Benzonia, Michigan)
Originated by: Jim Conkright
Tied by: Jim Conkright

Hook: Mustad 37160, #6-#12
Thread: Brown or black
Tail: Pheasant tail or other brown fibers
Body: Latex cut to 1/8" strip, wrapped, and colored with waterproof marker: belly is golden yellow, back is brown
Ribbing: Brown hackle, clipped short on top and sides

Comments: This fly can be fished for trout, steelhead, and salmon and is particularly productive on the Betsie and Platte rivers in Michigan. It can also be tied in a variety of colors for use as an attractor pattern.

Maple Syrup

Pattern type: Green drake nymph, dragonfly nymph, hellgrammite
Submitted by: Theriault Flies (Patten, Maine)
Originated by: Alvin Theriault adaptation of chenille nymph
Tied by: Holly Theriault

Hook: Mustad 3665A, #10
Thread: Black 6/0 prewaxed
Tail: Yellow calf tail
Body: Beige #2 chenille

Comments: This fly is tied for trout and landlocked salmon on both lakes and rivers. It is fished as a nymph. The body on this pattern should be thickly tied; trout, Theriault explains, will hold on to the fly longer and produce more hook-ups.

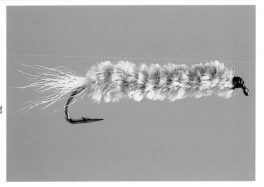

Philoplume Hare's Ear (Natural)

Pattern type: Mayfly nymph, caddis
Submitted by: River's Edge Fly Shop (Thunder Bay, Ontario)
Originated by: Bill Boote
Tied by: Romeo Rancourt

Hook: Daiichi 1530, #8-#14; weight optional
Thread: Black Danville 6/0
Tail: Philoplume (aftershaft) from pheasant rump
Body: Natural hare's ear dubbing
Ribbing: Pearl Krystal Flash, counterwrapped
Hackle: Aftershaft from pheasant rump, palmered over thorax
Wing case: Peacock herl

Philoplume Hare's Ear (Olive)

Pattern type: Mayfly nymph, caddis
Submitted by: River's Edge Fly Shop (Thunder Bay, Ontario)
Originated by: Bill Boote
Tied by: Romeo Rancourt

Hook: Daiichi 1530, #8-#14; weight optional
Thread: Olive Danville 6/0
Tail: Dyed olive philoplume (aftershaft) from pheasant rump
Body: Olive hare's ear dubbing
Ribbing: Pearl Krystal Flash, counterwrapped
Hackle: Dyed olive aftershaft from pheasant rump, palmered over thorax
Wing case: Peacock herl

Red Eye Gravy

Pattern type: Mayfly nymph
Submitted by: The Fish Hawk (Atlanta, Georgia)
Originated by: Robert Rooks, Jr.
Tied by: Robert Rooks, Jr.

Hook: TMC 206BL, #16-#20
Thread: Camel UNI 8/0
Tail: Hungarian partridge saddle feather fibers
Body: SLF HM7 brown/olive baetis dubbing
Legs: Hungarian partridge saddle feather
Head: Small red glass bead

Comments: "This non-descript nymph," says Robert Rooks, "is a great dropper fly."

Shannon's No. 1

Top view

Bottom view

Pattern type: Quill Gordon (*Epeorus pleuralis*) nymph
Submitted by: Les Shannon's Fly & Tackle Shop (Califon, New Jersey)
Originated by: Les Shannon
Tied by: Les Shannon

Hook: Partridge Flat-Bodied Nymph Hook H3ST, #16; or Mustad 3906B, #12
Thread: Brown 6/0 pre-waxed
Tail: 2 moose body hairs spread at 45-degree angle
Body: Dubbing blend of 70% gray fox mask fur, 15% olive rabbit, 15% brown rabbit
Gills: Light dun ostrich herl wrapped around front 2/3 of abdomen
Wing case: Dark mottled turkey feather
Legs: English grouse or brown partridge tied on each side (or substitute speckled hen back)

Comments: "I first tied this fly in 1957," explains Les Shannon, "long before I could identify the natural insect. This is how the names of my earlier patterns came about— they were numbered instead of named. It was not until I opened my fly shop in 1973 that my name was attached to the number. I will fish this pattern several hours before the hatch starts, then switch to a standard Gold-ribbed Hare's Ear nymph, but one tied with the same dubbing blend as described here."

Shannon's No. 3

Top view

Pattern type: Isonychia (*bicolor, saddleri, harperi*) nymph
Submitted by: Les Shannon's Fly & Tackle Shop (Califon, New Jersey)
Originated by: Les Shannon
Tied by: Les Shannon

Hook: Partridge Flat-Bodied Nymph Hook H3ST, #16; or Mustad 9671, #8-#12
Thread: Black 6/0 pre-waxed
Tail: 3 moose body hairs
Body: Dubbing blend of 50% claret rabbit fur, 50% dark brown rabbit fur
Gills: Black ostrich herl laid along sides before ribbing
Ribbing: Black cotton thread or gray Translucent Nylon thread
Wing case: Black goose or turkey quill
Legs: English grouse or brown partridge tied on each side (or substitute speckled hen back)

Comments: "To imitate *Isonychia saddleri*," Les Shannon notes, "I will fish this pattern in the riffles near the bottom, several hours before the hatch starts, and then switch to a twitching/rising motion as emergence occurs."

Soft Hackle Beadhead Pheasant Tail

Pattern type:	Mayfly nymph
Submitted by:	Dakota Angler & Outfitter (Rapid City, South Dakota)
Originated by:	Jim Smoragiewicz variation of Pheasant Tail Nymph
Tied by:	Jim Smoragiewicz
Hook:	TMC 2457, #16
Thread:	Brown or black Benecchi 10/0
Tail:	Pheasant tail fibers
Abdomen:	Pheasant tail fibers
Ribbing:	Copper wire, counterwrapped
Wing case:	Pheasant tail fibers
Thorax:	Peacock herl or Arizona Peacock dubbing
Hackle:	Starling
Head:	Gold metal bead

Comments: Tyer Jim Smoragiewicz notes, "I feel the key to the great success I have had with this pattern over other Pheasant Tail nymphs is the shape it gets from the curved hook and the movement the starling hackle gives to the fly. I have been fishing this pattern since 1992."

South Fork Drifter

Top view

Pattern type:	Ephemerella (subvaria, rotunda, invaria, dorothea, etc.) nymph
Submitted by:	Adventure Fly Fishing (Greensboro, North Carolina)
Originated by:	Jeff Wilkins
Tied by:	Jeff Wilkins
Hook:	Orvis 1639, #12-#18
Thread:	Black or tobacco brown UNI 8/0
Tail:	Pheasant tail fibers
Abdomen:	4-5 pheasant fibers for hooks #12-#14; 3-4 fibers for hooks #16-#18
Ribbing:	Danville Monothread or gold wire, counterwrapped
Wing case:	Pheasant tail fibers, 8-12 depending on hook size
Thorax:	Dark stone Umpqua Sparkleblend dubbing (or substitute Antron dubbing)
Legs:	Black or brown hen hackle, brushed with toothbrush to soften fibers
Head:	Pheasant tail fibers from wing case, doubled back and tied down

Comments: Jeff Wilkins explains, "This pattern was developed to match the Sulphur/Hendrickson group of mayflies so widespread in our area. This group represents one of the two major types of mayflies that produce reliable hatches. This pattern can be varied to match the color of the natural simply by changing the color of pheasant tail fibers that are used. We use this nymph for sight-fishing to cruising, shallow-water nymph feeders on Tennessee's South Holston River. It is a deadly spring pattern." The darker version in the main photograph is an imitation of the invaria/rotunda species; the lighter version in the supplementary photo represents Ephemerella dorothea.

Sparkle Hex Nymph

Pattern type:	Hexagenia limbata nymph, general attractor
Submitted by:	Backcast Fly Shop (Benzonia, Michigan)
Originated by:	Jim Empie
Tied by:	Jim Empie
Hook:	Mustad 3399A, #6-#8
Thread:	Tan or beige
Tail:	Pheasant tail fibers
Abdomen:	Tan or brown sparkle yarn encircling the tail and tied off around tail fibers
Thorax:	Cream or golden yellow yarn or dubbing
Wing case:	Sparkle yarn from abdomen pulled over top of thorax
Legs:	Variegated hen or Spey hackle—furnace, ginger, or dyed tan
Eyes:	Extra-small mono eyes

Comments: The extended-body style gives this fly more movement in the water.

Swimming Hexagenia Nymph

Pattern type: *Hexagenia limbata* nymph
Submitted by: Backcast Fly Shop (Benzonia, Michigan)
Originated by: unknown
Tied by: Holly Flies

Hook: TMC 200R, #4-#10
Thread: Tan or cream
Tail: White feather barbs or pheasant tail fibers
Body: Tan/gold yarn or dubbing
Ribbing: Tan or cream thread
Gills: Tan, gray, or brown aftershaft
Shellback/
Wing case: Turkey quill
Legs: Natural bird body feather—partridge, pheasant, etc.

Top view

Tan Tellico

Pattern type: *Stenonema* nymph
Submitted by: Fly Angler (Fridley, Minnesota)
Originated by: Chris Hansen version of traditional Tellico
Tied by: Chris Hansen

Hook: 2XL nymph, #12-#14
Thread: Brown 6/0
Tail: Pheasant tail fibers
Body: Tan floss
Ribbing: Peacock herl
Shellback: Pheasant tail fibers from tail
Hackle: Brown

Comments: Chris Hansen notes, "The Tellico has always been a good nymph for me, and this variation seems to work particularly well on the Rush River in Wisconsin. I think it does a good job of imitating the *Stenonema* nymphs found there."

TCO Antron Back Nymph (Sulphur)

Other versions clockwise from upper left:
olive, dark brown, dark gray, light gray

Pattern type: Sulphur nymph
Submitted by: Tulpehocken Creek Outfitters
(Reading, Pennsylvania)
Originated by: Tony Gehman and
Dave Eshenower
Tied by: Tony Gehman and
Dave Eshenower

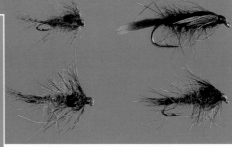

Hook: TMC 100, #12-#20
Thread: Rusty dun UNI 8/0
Tail: Mottled hen back fibers
Body: Sulphur yellow TCO
East Coast
Nymph Dubbing
Wing case: Brown Antron
Legs: Mottled hen back fibers

Comments: Tony Gehman and Dave Eshenower explain, "We designed this series of flies because we feel a nymph needs to be buggy! A tightly wrapped fly doesn't breathe and move in the water. The incorporation of Antron gives these flies the right amount of shimmer."

TP's Hex Nymph

Pattern type: *Hexagenia* nymph
Submitted by: Bob Mitchell's Fly Shop (Lake Elmo, Minnesota)
Originated by: Tracy Peterson
Tied by: Tracy Peterson

Hook: TMC 300, #8; lead wire lashed along top of shank so hook
rides point-up
Thread: Yellow 6/0
Tail: Ginger marabou
Body: Ginger ostrich herl
Shellback: Peacock herl
Ribbing: Medium copper wire
Hackle: Ginger hen saddle
Wing case: Peacock herl from shellback

Top view

Two Tone Nymph

Top view

Pattern type: Mayfly nymph
Submitted by: Adventure Fly Fishing
(Greensboro, North Carolina)
Originated by: Jeff Wilkins
Tied by: Jeff Wilkins

Hook: TMC 3769 or TMC 100, #16-#18
Thread: Black UNI 8/0
Tail: Black Micro Fibbets
Abdomen: Olive brown turkey biot
Ribbing: Danville Monothread or 5x tippet material
Shellback: 1/2 strand black Z-lon
Thorax: Olive brown Angora dubbing
Legs: 4-6 strands black Z-lon tied in with figure-8 wraps
Wing case: Black turkey biot mounted behind hook eye, coated with black Loon Hardhead Fly Finish

Bottom view

Comments: "The Two Tone Nymph," explains tyer Jeff Wilkins, "is used for both early-season BWOs—most notably the *Paraleptophlebia* (blue quill) and some of the smaller BWOs which hatch later in spring and through early summer. It can be fished on the bottom as with any other nymph, but is deadly when tied unweighted and fished upstream to rising fish (on a greased line or under a small indicator). It will score on many of those fish that snub a surface offering." Note that the biot for the abdomen is tied in so that wrapping it raises the fringe-like barbules to form a rib.

Unusual Nymph

Pattern type: Mayfly nymph
Submitted by: The Forks Fly Shop (Inglewood, Ontario)
Originated by: Wayne F. Martin
Tied by: Wayne F. Martin

Hook: Partridge K4A Grub, #10-#18; weight optional
Thread: Black
Tail: Emu fibers
Abdomen: Hare's ear dubbing (with guard hairs)
Ribbing: Fine copper wire, counterwrapped
Thorax: Fitch underfur, picked out
Wing case: Deer hair, mounted at eye and secured at rear of thorax, trimmed to leave stubble at rear, lacquered

Comments: Wayne Martin polishes the copper ribbing wire with car wax to maintain brightness. The fly should be fished with a slight action.

Wiggle Hex

Pattern type: *Hexagenia limbata* nymph
Submitted by: Riverbend Sport Shop
(Southfield, Michigan)
Originated by: unknown
Tied by: Matt Reid

Bottom view

Hook: TMC 200R, #8-#10
Thread: Brown or tan 6/0
Tail: Brown or tan webby hackle fibers
Abdomen: Wiggle extension—cream Antron on length of floral wire
Front hook—bronze Antron mixture
Wing case: Mottled oak Wapsi Thinskin
Thorax: Cream Antron
Legs: Brown webby hackle fibers, tied in 2 pairs
Eyes: Black mono eyes
Antennae: Brown webby hackle fibers

Comments: The body extension here is tied on a length of floral wire, doubled over to form a loop eye. This eye is connected to the front hook by a loop of monofilament lashed to the shank of the front hook.

X

Pattern type: *Hexagenia* and *Ephemera* nymph, general attractor
Submitted by: Thornapple Orvis Shop (Grand Rapids, Michigan)
Originated by: Dave Hise
Tied by: Dave Hise

Hook: Eagle Claw L7042G, #6-#8
Thread: Tan UNI 6/0
Tail (opt.): Emu fibers
Abdomen: Tan chenille, small
Shellback: Clear Bodi-Stretch
Ribbing: Fine copper wire
Thorax: Pearl-olive Estaz
Legs: Tan/gray emu palmered over thorax
Wing case: Clear Bodi-Stretch from shellback

Comments: Dave Hise notes, "This fly is very productive throughout the year in rivers with good populations of Ephemeridae. It is especially productive during high-water periods when these burrowing nymphs are kicked up into the current. It's effective on both trout and steelhead in the Muskegon, Rogue, and Pere Marquette rivers."

Emergers

Bead Head Rabbit Emerger (Sulphur)

Pattern type: Sulphur emerger
Submitted by: Adventure Fly Fishing (Greensboro, North Carolina)
Originated by: Jeff Wilkins
Tied by: Jeff Wilkins

Hook: TMC 2302, #14-#18
Thread: Yellow UNI 8/0
Shuck: Brown Z-lon
Abdomen: Pheasant tail fibers
Ribbing: Copper wire, counterwrapped
Thorax: Superfine PMD dubbing
Wing case: Snowshoe rabbit's foot
Hackle: Ginger or light dun hen, 2-3 turns
Head: Gold bead

Biot Sulphur Emerger

Pattern type: Sulphur emerger
Submitted by: Adventure Fly Fishing (Greensboro, North Carolina)
Originated by: Jeff Wilkins
Tied by: Jeff Wilkins

Hook: Mustad 94840, #14-#18
Thread: Yellow UNI 8/0
Shuck: Olive brown Z-lon
Abdomen: Yellow turkey biot
Ribbing: Stripped yellow hackle stem
Thorax: Superfine sulphur orange dubbing
Legs: 6 strands clear Antron yarn in center of thorax
Wing: Snowshoe rabbit's foot

Blue Dun Emerger

Pattern type: *Baetis* emerger
Submitted by: Bob Mitchell's Fly Shop (Lake Elmo, Minnesota)
Originated by: Michael Alwin
Tied by: Michael Alwin

Hook: TMC 3761, #18
Thread: Gray UNI 8/0
Tail: Wood duck flank fibers
Body: Gray Antron or Antron/rabbit dubbing
Wing: Wild turkey marabou

Comments: This fly is fished down-and-across, both before and during emergence.

Bob's Baetis

Pattern type: *Baetis* emerger
Submitted by: Oak Orchard Fly Shop (Williamsville, New York)
Originated by: Bob Morrissey
Tied by: Bob Morrissey

Hook: TMC 101, #24
Thread: Olive UNI 8/0
Shuck: Grizzly rooster neck tip dyed olive
Abdomen: Olive tying thread
Thorax: Peacock herl
Wings: 2 dark dun hen hackle tips
Hackle: Dark dun neck hackle, 2 turns, trimmed flat on top and bottom

Front view

Comments: "The trailing shuck on this pattern," notes tyer Bob Morrissey, "is one cock cape tip. If left untreated with floatant, the hackle tip is a damp material—never too wet or too dry—the perfect material to keep the fly right in the surface film." This pattern has proven effective on streams in both the East and West.

Bob's Emerger

Pattern type: *Ephemerella* emerger (sulphur version)
Submitted by: Oak Orchard Fly Shop (Williamsville, New York)
Originated by: Bob Morrissey
Tied by: Bob Morrissey

Hook: TMC 205BL, #20
Thread: Rusty Dun UNI 8/0
Tail: 4-5 fibers of Harrop brown marabou
Abdomen: marabou from tail, twisted and wrapped
Thorax: Sulphur orange East Coast dubbing
Wings: 2 medium dun CDC tips flanked by 2 light dun hen hackle tips
Legs: Medium dun CDC fibers

Front view

Comments: Like Bob's Ephemerger (below) and Bob's Baetis (above), this pattern combines wet and dry materials to position the fly properly on the water. This pattern, Bob Morrissey observes, has been successful on wild trout from the streams of New York and Pennsylvania to Silver Creek and Henrys Fork.

Bob's Ephemerger

Pattern type: *Ephemerella* emerger (*subvaria* version)
Submitted by: Oak Orchard Fly Shop (Williamsville, New York)
Originated by: Bob Morrissey
Tied by: Bob Morrissey

Hook: TMC 2487, #14
Thread: Rusty dun UNI 8/0
Tail: 4-5 fibers of Harrop brown marabou
Abdomen: Marabou from tail, twisted and wrapped
Thorax: Red quill East Coast dubbing
Collar: Clipped butts of deer hair wing
Hackle: Dark dun Hoffman neck hackle, 2 turns behind wing, 1 in front
Wing: Dark dun deer hair

Comments: This fly represents tyer Bob Morrissey's approach to combining wet and dry materials to give a pattern a more natural appearance and position on the water (see also Bob's Emerger and Bob's Baetis, above). Morrissey traces this approach to Rene Harrop, Bob Quigley, Mike Lawson, Shane Stalcup, and back to early ideas of Vince Marinaro. Absorbent materials cause the rear portion of the fly to sink, while deer hair and hackle at the front (not treated with floatant) hold the forward portion of the pattern on the surface. He says, "This pattern is the most productive emerger I have ever fished, from the Delaware River to Pennsylvania's spring creeks. I have observed hundred of *Ephemerella* emergences, and this fly is an exact imitation of the mayfly as it first breaks the surface film and struggles from its nymphal shuck."

CDC Pop Emerger
(Blue-Winged Olive)

Front view

Pattern type: Blue-winged olive emerger
Submitted by: Tulpehocken Creek Outfitters (Reading, Pennsylvania)
Originated by: Tony Gehman and Dave Eshenower
Tied by: Tony Gehman and Dave Eshenower

Hook: TMC 2487, #14-#26
Thread: Rusty dun UNI 8/0
Tail: Wood duck flank fibers
Body: Blue winged olive TCO East Coast Dubbing
Wing: TCO natural CDC, tied facing forward

Comments: "This pattern," note tyers Tony Gehman and Dave Eshenower, "is not only one of our most popular patterns, it may be the most effective emerger we've ever fished. This fly is designed to imitate a mayfly struggling to pop through the surface tension. The body extends down through the surface film into the water, unlike most other emergers, while the CDC wing keeps the fly buoyant and visible."

CDC Pop Emerger (Sulphur)

Pattern type: Sulphur emerger (*Ephemerella invaria* or *dorothea*)
Submitted by: Tulpehocken Creek Outfitters (Reading, Pennsylvania)
Originated by: Tony Gehman and Dave Eshenower
Tied by: Tony Gehman and Dave Eshenower

Hook: TMC 2487, #14-#20
Thread: Rusty dun UNI 8/0
Tail: Wood duck flank fibers
Abdomen: Sulphur spinner TCO East Coast Dubbing
Wing: TCO natural CDC, tied facing forward
Thorax: Sulphur yellow TCO East Coast Dubbing

CDC Pop Emerger (Trico)

Pattern type: Trico emerger
Submitted by: Tulpehocken Creek Outfitters (Reading, Pennsylvania)
Originated by: Tony Gehman and Dave Eshenower
Tied by: Tony Gehman and Dave Eshenower

Hook: TMC 2487, #20-#26
Thread: UNI 17/0
Tail: Wood duck flank fibers
Abdomen: Trico abdomen TCO East Coast Dubbing
Wings: TCO natural CDC, tied facing forward
Thorax: Trico thorax TCO East Coast Dubbing

Dammit Emerger (BWO)

Pattern type: Blue-winged olive emerger
Submitted by: Choo Choo Fly & Tackle (Chattanooga, Tennessee)
Originated by: Brad Weeks
Tied by: Brad Weeks

Hook: TMC 3487, #16-#18
Thread: Olive dun 8/0
Tail: 3 pheasant tail fibers
Abdomen: Pheasant tail fibers dyed olive
Ribbing: Fine gold wire
Thorax: Olive dubbing
Wing: Dun poly yarn
Hackle: Dun

Dammit Emerger (Sulphur)

Pattern type: Sulphur emerger
Submitted by: Choo Choo Fly & Tackle (Chattanooga, Tennessee)
Originated by: Brad Weeks
Tied by: Brad Weeks

Hook: TMC 3487, #14-#18
Thread: Light Cahill 8/0
Tail: 3 pheasant tail fibers
Abdomen: Pheasant tail fibers
Ribbing: Fine gold wire
Thorax: Sulphur dubbing (Beck's dubbing blend)
Wing: Light dun poly yarn
Hackle: Ginger

DS Emerger

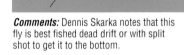

Pattern type: Mayfly emerger/nymph
Submitted by: Catskill Flies (Roscoe, New York)
Originated by: Dennis Skarka
Tied by: Dennis Skarka

Hook: TMC 2487, #12-#18
Thread: Olive
Tail: Brown Antron yarn
Body: Dubbing of equal parts brown, claret, and gray furs
Wing case: Light gray poly yarn
Legs (opt.): Partridge hackle

Top view

Comments: Dennis Skarka notes that this fly is best fished dead drift or with split shot to get it to the bottom.

Evergreen Crystal Emerger (BWO)

Pattern type: Blue-winged olive emerger
Submitted by: Evergreen Fly Fishing Company (Clarksburg, West Virginia)
Originated by: Franklin Oliverio
Tied by: Ken Long

Hook: Dry fly, #14-#18
Thread: Olive 8/0
Shuck: White or pale yellow Z-lon
Abdomen: Olive turkey biot
Wing: Pearl Krystal Flash
Thorax: Olive natural or synthetic dubbing
Hackle: Grizzly

Comments: The Krystal Flash wing makes this low-floating pattern more visible to the angler. The biot that forms that abdomen on this fly is wrapped so that the fringe of barbules is exposed to form ribbing segmentation. The thorax should be rather plump.

Evergreen Crystal Emerger (Sulphur)

Pattern type: Sulphur mayfly emerger
Submitted by: Evergreen Fly Fishing Company (Clarksburg, West Virginia)
Originated by: Franklin Oliverio
Tied by: Ken Long

Hook: Dry fly, #14-#18
Thread: White or yellow 8/0
Shuck: Whilte or pale yellow Z-lon
Abdomen: Orange-sulphur turkey biot
Wing: Pear Krystal Flash
Thorax: Orange-sulphur natural or synthetic dubbing
Hackle: Grizzly

Comments: Like the blue-winged olive version, this pattern uses a turkey biot wrapped to give a fringe-like ribbing to the abdomen.

Green Drake Emerger

Pattern type:	Green drake emerger
Submitted by:	Theriault Flies (Patten, Maine)
Originated by:	Alvin Theriault
Tied by:	Connie Theriault

Hook:	Mustad 37160, #10
Thread:	Black 6/0 prewaxed
Body:	#18 or #19 Swannundaze
Downwing:	Olive calf tail
Upright wings:	Olive calf tail tied Wulff style
Hackle:	One olive and one grizzly

Front view

Comments: On this pattern, the rear portion of the body sinks beneath the surface film, while the front portion floats. Fish it dead drift.

Half 'N' Half Emerger

Pattern type:	Mayfly emerger (sulphur version)
Submitted by:	Adventure Fly Fishing (Greensboro, North Carolina)
Originated by:	Jeff Wilkins
Tied by:	Jeff Wilkins

Hook:	Orvis 1639, #12-#18
Thread:	White UNI 8/0
Shuck:	Olive brown Z-lon
Abdomen:	4 pheasant tail fibers
Ribbing:	Copper wire, counterwrapped
Thorax:	Silver glass bead followed by yellow Superfine Dry Fly dubbing
Legs:	Yellow CDC, 2-3 turns palmered over thorax
Wing:	Light coastal deer hair, stacked

Comments: "This emerger pattern," explains tyer Jeff Wilkins, "was developed for fishing the Sulphur and Hendrickson hatches on the tailwater rivers of eastern Tennessee. The Half 'N' Half name comes from the position of this fly on the water; it sits with the rear half of the body beneath the surface. The CDC encourages air bubbles to form around the fly. It works well with or without the thorax bead."

Jay's Olive Emerger (Floating)

Pattern type:	Blue-winged olive emerger
Submitted by:	Coleman's Fly Shop (Spencerport, New York)
Originated by:	Jay Peck
Tied by:	Jay Peck

Hook:	Daiichi 1710, #16
Thread:	Olive UNI 8/0
Tail:	Brown partridge fibers
Body:	Medium olive dubbing
Wing case:	White closed-cell craft foam colored dark gray with waterproof marker
Legs:	Brown partridge fibers

Comments: This fly is fished dead drift to feeding trout.

Jay's Sulphur Emerger

Pattern type:	Sulphur emerger
Submitted by:	Coleman's Fly Shop (Spencerport, New York)
Originated by:	Jay Peck
Tied by:	Jay Peck

Hook:	Daiichi 1150, #16
Thread:	Yellow UNI 8/0
Shuck:	Dark brown Z-lon
Body:	Sulphur yellow rabbit fur
Ribbing:	Fine gold wire
Wing:	Loop of dun hen hackle fibers

Comments: This pattern is fished dead drift in the surface film and can be given an occasional twitch.

John's Sulfur Emerger

Pattern type: Sulphur emerger
Submitted by: Coleman's Fly Shop (Spencerport, New York)
Originated by: John Abiuso
Tied by: John Abiuso

Hook: Daiichi 1150 scud/caddis, #16
Thread: Primrose UNI 8/0
Shuck: Brown Antron mixed with mallard flank fibers
Body: Sulphur yellow dubbing, fine
Ribbing: Fine gold wire, counterwrapped
Wing: Coastal elk

Comments: John Abiuso notes, "This fly was designed for the selective browns of Spring Creek in Mumford, New York. Fish it upstream with an occasional twitch to imitate the emerging insect. Grease the wing to keep it floating in the surface film."

Low Rider Emerger
(BWO)

Pattern type: Blue-winged olive emerger
Submitted by: Choo Choo Fly & Tackle (Chattanooga, Tennessee)
Originated by: Ryan Meulemans
Tied by: Ryan Meulemans

Hook: TMC 5210, #16-#20
Thread: Olive 8/0
Tail: Brown Z-lon
Abdomen: Pheasant tail
Ribbing: Fine copper wire
Thorax: Olive dubbing
Wing case: White closed-cell foam
Hackle: Dun

Top view

Bottom view

Low Rider Emerger
(Sulphur)

Pattern type: Sulphur emerger
Submitted by: Choo Choo Fly & Tackle (Chattanooga, Tennessee)
Originated by: Ryan Meulemans
Tied by: Ryan Meulemans

Hook: TMC 5210, #14-#20
Thread: Pale yellow 8/0
Tail: Brown Z-lon
Abdomen: Pheasant tail fibers
Ribbing: Fine copper wire
Thorax: Pale yellow dubbing
Wing case: White closed-cell foam
Hackle: Ginger

Top view

Bottom view

Poly Quigley (BWO)

Pattern type: Blue-winged olive emerger
Submitted by: The Fish Hawk (Atlanta, Georgia)
Originated by: Jason Farmer adaptation of Bob Quigley pattern
Tied by: Robert Rooks, Jr.

Hook: TMC 100 or TMC 2487, #16
Thread: Olive dun UNI 8/0
Shuck: Olive brown Antron or Z-lon, or color to match natural
Body: Blue-winged olive Nature's Spirit dubbing, or color to match natural
Wings: Light gray poly yarn
Hackle: Dun

Comments: When he was guiding, Jason Farmer began dressing Quigley Cripples with a yarn wing and dubbed body to speed up the tying. Sizes and colors can be altered to match a variety of mayfly species.

QD Mayfly Emerger/Stillborn

Front view

Pattern type: Mayfly emerger/stillborn
Submitted by: Great Lakes Fly Fishing Company (Rockford, Michigan)
Originated by: Bob Braendle
Tied by: Bob Braendle

Hook: TMC 200R, #16 or size to match natural
Thread: Gray or color to match natural
Tail: Mallard flank fibers
Shuck: Rust Antron, Darlon, or Z-lon, or color to match natural; tied in at rear of hook and pulled forward over body
Body: Light brown Superfine dubbing or color to match natural
Hackle: 3-4 wraps grizzly dyed brown or olive or color to match natural, clipped top and bottom
Wings: Gray poly yarn (or deer hair or snowshoe rabbit)

Red Quill Emerger

Pattern type: Mayfly emerger, general attractor
Submitted by: Delaware River Anglers (Willow Grove, Pennsylvania)
Originated by: Ken Schwam
Tied by: Ken Schwam

Hook: Mustad 3906B, #12
Thread: Olive 6/0 Danville
Tail: 3-6 wood duck flank fibers
Abdomen: Stripped brown hackle quill over sparse hare's ear underbody
Thorax: Hare's ear dubbing
Wings: Mallard quill
Hackle: Hungarian partridge, sparse

Comments: "This fly," says Ken Schwam, "was originally tied to take fish during the Hendrickson hatch, but it has proven to be an excellent searching pattern on all trout waters. It should be fished on the swing, like a wet fly, or dead-drifted along the bottom. I often fish this fly in pairs and get rising fish to take it. Don't fish this fly on anything lighter than 4x or you risk a broken tippet."

Rivergod Emerger
(Hendrickson version)

Front view

Pattern type: Mayfly emerger
Submitted by: Great Lakes Fly Fishing Company (Rockford, Michigan)
Originated by: Dennis M. Potter
Tied by: Dennis M. Potter

Hook: TMC 100, #12-#20; TMC 2488, #22-#24
Thread: 8/0 to match natural
Tail: Wood duck flank fibers
Shuck: Hi Vis wing material, 2/3 length of tail (hooks #20 and smaller, no shuck)
Body: Hooks #12-#14, dubbing to match natural; hooks #16 and smaller, tying thread to match natural
Wings: Dark dun crinkled Z-lon

Comments: This fly design can be tied to match many hatches and has proven effective all over the country. Hooks #16 and smaller use a thread body, but have a dubbed thorax with one turn of dubbing behind the wing and the remainder in front of the wing.

Top: Slate wing olive version; lower left: sulphur/PMD version; lower right blue-winged olive version

Rose's Sulphur Emerger

Front view

Pattern type: Sulphur emerger
Submitted by: Coleman's Fly Shop (Spencerport, New York)
Originated by: Gary Rose
Tied by: Rick Tabor

Hook: Daiichi 1150 or Daiichi 1130, #14-#18
Thread: Yellow 6/0 or 8/0
Tail: Medium blue dun ostrich herl or hen hackle tip
Abdomen: Sulphur yellow rabbit fur
Ribbing: 1 strand of yellow Krystal Flash
Wing: Slate gray CDC feather or puff
Thorax/Head: Sulphur yellow rabbit fur tinted with small amount of chartreuse rabbit fur

Streamside Mahogany

Pattern type: *Isonychia bicolor* emerger and spinner
Submitted by: Streamside Orvis (Williamsburg, Michigan)
Originated by: Mark Lord
Tied by: Mark Lord

Hook: Orvis Dry Fly 1523, #12
Thread: Gray 6/0
Tail: Dark brown fine elk hock or yearling elk
Body: Deer hair dyed claret, tips flared at rear
Ribbing: Tying thread crisscrossed over deer-hair body
Wing: Dun calf body or tail (or gray poly yarn or Z-lon)
Hackle: Grizzly

Comments: This pattern does double duty, as an emerger and a spinner. Orvis Streamside dyes its own deer hair to a claret color. Mark Lord indicates that a dark red deer hair can be substituted for the body if desired.

Vertical Emerger—
Parachute Hendrickson

Version with CDC loop wing

Pattern type: Hendrickson emerger
Submitted by: Housatonic River Outfitters (West Cornwall, Connecticut)
Originated by: Harold McMillan
Tied by: Harold McMillan

Hook: TMC 400T, #12-#14
Thread: Airflo wine 14/0
Shuck: Brown Darlon
Abdomen: Brown dubbing, blend of synthetic, rabbit, and squirrel
Ribbing: Gold wire
Thorax: Hendrickson blend to match natural
Wingpost: White calf body hair
Hackle: Light dun Hoffman

Comments: This unusual emerger is designed to ride with the body submerged, while the wing floats in the surface film. In addition to the standard parachute-hackle version, Harold McMillan ties the two other variations pictured here. One has a wing formed from a pair of mallard gray CDC feathers, tied in a loop behind the hook eye. The other has a wing formed from a tuft of rabbit's foot hair, hand-tinted a light gray. For the thorax portion of the fly, McMillan prefers a Hendrickson dubbing blend of rabbit and mole that is mixed and dyed by tyer Del Mazza. Hook size and body color can be altered to match a variety of mayfly and caddis species.

Version with rabbit's-foot wing

Duns

Aroostook Blue Wing Olive

Pattern type:	Blue-winged olive dun
Submitted by:	Thom's of Maine (Houlton, Maine)
Originated by:	Thom Willard
Tied by:	Thom Willard

Hook:	TMC 101, #16-#22
Thread:	Olive UNI 8/0
Tail:	Moose neck hair, bleached and dyed dun
Body:	Turkey biot, dyed olive over yellow
Wings:	Dun hen hackle tips
Hackle:	Dark dun

Berge's Bullethead Hex

Pattern type:	*Hexagenia limbata* dun
Submitted by:	The Superior Fly Angler (Superior, Wisconsin)
Originated by:	Dick Berge
Tied by:	Dick Berge

Hook:	Mustad 94840 or TMC 100, #6-#8
Thread:	Yellow Flymaster Plus
Tail:	Moose body hair
Body:	Pale yellow deer hair
Ribbing:	Yellow Flymaster Plus
Wings:	Natural deer hair tips from head
Head:	Natural deer hair, bullet style

Biot Loop Wing BWO

Pattern type:	Blue-winged olive dun
Submitted by:	Dakota Angler & Outfitter (Rapid City, South Dakota)
Originated by:	Hans Stephenson
Tied by:	Hans Stephenson

Hook:	Partridge L3B or similar up-eye dry-fly hook, #18-#20
Thread:	Light dun 12/0
Tail:	Nutria guard hairs, tied split
Body:	Olive silk dubbing
Wing:	Light dun goose biot
Legs:	Dun CDC puffs

Comments: "This fly works best," Hans Stephenson says, "when waterproofed with Hareline Watershed or a similar product."

Black Mayfly

Pattern type:	Mayfly dun
Submitted by:	Corey's Handtied Flies (Yarmouth, Nova Scotia)
Originated by:	unknown
Tied by:	Corey Burke

Hook:	Mustad 7948A, #14-#18
Thread:	Black UNI 8/0
Tail:	3-4 strands dark moose hair
Body:	Black tying thread
Ribbing:	Very fine silver or gold wire
Hackle:	Black

Comments: This is a productive pattern for April and May hatches or when the blackflies are thick.

Blue-Winged Olive CDC Loop-wing Dun

Pattern type:	Blue-winged olive dun
Submitted by:	Mountain Valley Flies (Solon, Maine)
Originated by:	John Kenealy
Tied by:	John Kenealy
Hook:	Mustad 94840 or other standard dry-fly, #14-#22
Thread:	Olive 6/0 or 8/0
Tail:	Medium dun hackle fibers
Body:	Light olive beaver dubbing
Wings:	Slate-colored CDC feather

Front view

Comments: Tyer John Kenealy designed this fly for the BWO hatch on Maine's Kennebec River. To form the wing, tie in a CDC feather by the tip ahead of the dubbed abdomen. Apply a small amount of dubbing over the tie-in point. Fold the feather forward to make a loop, secure the feather, and clip. Dub a head. The CDC can be trimmed to help even out the shape of the wing. Sizes and colors of this design can be altered to match a variety of mayfly species.

Borcher Special

Pattern type:	Mayfly dun
Submitted by:	Backcast Fly Shop (Benzonia, Michigan)
Originated by:	unknown
Tied by:	Holly Flies
Hook:	Mustad 94840, #10-#16
Thread:	Black
Tail:	Pheasant tail fibers
Body:	Mottled turkey wing quill fibers
Wings:	Dun, cream, or white hackle tips
Hackle:	Brown and grizzly mixed.

Front view

Comments: Depending on size, this pattern can imitate a variety of mayfly species.

CDC No-Hackle Dun
(Blue-Winged Olive)

Pattern type:	Blue-winged olive dun
Submitted by:	Tulpehocken Creek Outfitters (Reading, Pennsylvania)
Originated by:	Tony Gehman and Dave Eshenower
Tied by:	Tony Gehman and Dave Eshenower
Hook:	TMC 100, #14-#26
Thread:	Rusty dun UNI 8/0
Tail:	Dun Micro Fibetts
Body:	Blue-winged olive TCO East Coast Dubbing
Wings:	TCO natural CDC

Front view

Comments: Tyers Tony Gehman and Dave Eshenower note, "Our CDC No-Hackle Dun is a very realistic imiation that sits low in the surface film, yet is still very buoyant and visible. It is incredibly effective in a variety of water conditions, from riffles and pocket water to long, slow glides. Our tying technique utilizes the most buoyant part of the natural CDC feather (no stem—barbs only) and allows the wing to be full and long while remaining translucent and natural looking."

CDC No-Hackle Dun (Trico)

Pattern type:	Trico dun
Submitted by:	Tulpehocken Creek Outfitters Reading, Pennsylvania)
Originated by:	Tony Gehman and Dave Eshenower
Tied by:	Tony Gehman and Dave Eshenower
Hook:	TMC 2488, #20-#26
Thread:	UNI 17/0
Tail:	Dun Micro Fibetts
Abdomen:	Trico abdomen TCO East Coast Dubbing
Wings:	TCO natural CDC
Thorax:	Trico thorax TCO East Coast Dubbing

Comments: "We found it very difficult," observe Tony Gehman and Dave Eshenower, "to find any commercial patterns that would mimic our minute Trico species here on the East Coast. We incorporated our unique natural CDC to aid in floatation and visibility. These flies are tied on a short-shank, wide-gap hook."

CDC Puff

Pattern type: Blue-winged olive dun, olive midge, female Trico, emerging dun, caddis
Submitted by: The Sporting Gentleman (Media, Pennsylvania)
Originated by: Tom Fink
Tied by: Tom Fink

Hook: TMC 200R, #22; blackend with waterproof marker
Thread: Olive UNI 8/0
Tail: Olive brown Z-lon
Abdomen: Olive Kreinik silk dubbing
Wings: Slate/gray/blue CDC
Thorax: Peacock herl, sparse

Comments: Tyer Tom Fink colors the hook black before tying. The tail is made by splitting a Z-lon strand lengthwise, twisting a half-strand while simultaneously applying Blip floatant. The wing is formed from two CDC feathers, tied in by the tips at the winging point. The feather is then doubled over and bound down with 4 thread wraps. Additional thread wraps are used to post the wing in final position. The wing is then clipped to length. This fly has accounted for many large, fussy spring-creek trout.

CDC Thorax Dun
(Catskill Hendrickson)

Pattern type: Hendrickson dun (*Ephemerella subvaria*)
Submitted by: Tulpehocken Creek Outfitters (Reading, Pennsylvania)
Originated by: Tony Gehman and Dave Eshenower
Tied by: Tony Gehman and Dave Eshenower

Hook: TMC 100, #12-#16
Thread: Rusty dun UNI 8/0
Tail: Dun Micro Fibetts
Body: Catskill Hendriskson TCO East Coast Dubbing
Wings: TCO natural CDC
Hackle: Medium dun Hoffman saddle

Comments: Tony Gehman and Dave Eshenower point out, "This pattern is tied with a much darker abdomen than our standard Hendrickson due to the body coloration changes found on the West Branch, East Branch, and main stem of the Delaware River and other Catskill streams."

This pattern, and the versions that follow, were "designed to replace the standard turkey flat wing style. We found that CDC doesn't absorb as much water as a turkey-flat wing and is far more visible. We also cut the hackle in a 'V' shape underneath the fly so that it rides flush in the surface film."

CDC Thorax Dun
(Hendrickson Pink)

Pattern type: Hendrickson dun (*Ephemerella subvaria*)
Submitted by: Tulpehocken Creek Outfitters (Reading, Pennsylvania)
Originated by: Tony Gehman and Dave Eshenower
Tied by: Tony Gehman and Dave Eshenower

Hook: TMC 100, #12-#16
Thread: Rusty dun UNI 8/0
Tail: Dun Micro Fibetts
Body: Hendrickson pink TCO East Coast Dubbing
Wings: TCO natural CDC
Hackle: Medium dun Hoffman saddle, "V" clipped on bottom

CDC Thorax Dun (Slate Drake)

Pattern type: Slate drake dun (*Isonychia bicolor, saddleri,* or *harperi*)
Submitted by: Tulpehocken Creek Outfitters (Reading, Pennsylvania)
Originated by: Tony Gehman and Dave Eshenower
Tied by: Tony Gehman and Dave Eshenower

Hook: TMC 100, #12-#16
Thread: Rusty dun UNI 8/0
Tail: Dun Micro Fibetts
Body: *Isonychia* (slate drake) TCO East Coast Dubbing
Wings: TCO natural CDC
Hackle: Medium dun Hoffman saddle, "V" clipped on bottom

CDC Thorax Dun (Sulphur)

Front view

Pattern type: Sulphur dun (*Ephemerella invaria* or *dorothea*)
Submitted by: Tulpehocken Creek Outfitters
(Reading, Pennsylvania)
Originated by: Tony Gehman and Dave Eshenower
Tied by: Tony Gehman and Dave Eshenower

Hook: TMC 100, #14-#20
Thread: Rusty dun UNI 8/0
Tail: Dun Micro Fibetts
Body: Sulphur orange TCO East Coast Dubbing
Wings: TCO natural CDC
Hackle: Light dun Hoffman saddle, "V" clipped on bottom

Coleman's Male Hendrickson Oatka

Front view

Pattern type: Hendrickson dun
Submitted by: Coleman's Fly Shop
(Spencerport, New York)
Originated by: Carl Coleman
Tied by: Carl Coleman

Comments: This pattern can be fished dry or just under the surface with an occasional twitch. Trimming the hackle on the bottom lowers the body and gives this fly a more distinct profile.

Hook: Daiichi 1180, #14
Thread: Red UNI 8/0
Tail: Light dun Micro Fibetts
Body: Mad River #40 beaver dubbing mixed
with 20% Mad River #6 dubbing
Wings: Dark dun hen saddle feathers burned with Renzetti #402 wing burner
Hackle: Dark dun, 2 turns behind wing, 4 turns in front; clipped on bottom

Coleman's Sulfur Dun
(Spring Brook Oatka)

Front View

Pattern type: Sulphur dun
Submitted by: Coleman's Fly Shop
(Spencerport, New York)
Originated by: Carl Coleman
Tied by: Carl Coleman

Hook: Daiichi 1180, #16
Thread: Yellow UNI 8/0
Tail: Light ginger hackle fibers
Body: Light yellow rabbit fur
Wings: Light dun hen saddle burned with
Renzetti #402 wing burner
Hackle: 2 wraps light ginger behind wing, 4 in front of wing; clipped on bottom

Comments: This pattern dates back to 1963, when it was tied with cut wings.

Drew Mayfly

Comments: This brook trout pattern was originated for Garth Drew and was designed for visibility on the water. The rabbit's-foot wing reflects light, making the fly easier to see in the surface foam. The wing can be tied more heavily to increase visibility.

Pattern type: Mayfly adult
Submitted by: The Forks Fly Shop (Inglewood, Ontario)
Originated by: Wayne F. Martin
Tied by: Wayne F. Martin

Hook: TMC 103BL, #14-#20
Thread: Olive 8/0
Tail: 6-8 fitch tail guard hairs
Abdomen: Mixture 2/3 brown/olive rabbit dubbing,
1/3 dark tan #20 Fly Rite dubbing
Thorax: Mixture 1/2 abdomen dubbing, 1/2 dark tan #20 Fly Rite dubbing
Wing: Snowshoe rabbit foot, tied post style and slanted back
Hackle: Dark dun, 1 turn behind wing and 3 turns in front

Ephoron

Pattern type: *Ephoron* dun
Submitted by: Flies for Michigan (N. Muskegon, Michigan)
Originated by: Al Rockwood
Tied by: Al Rockwood

Hook: Mustad 94840, #14
Thread: White UNI 8/0
Tail: White porcupine guard hairs
Body: White UNI 8/0
Wing: White calf body
Thorax: White Superfine dubbing
Hackle: White

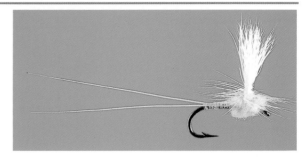

Comments: This pattern was designed to match the Ephoron hatch on the waters in the southern portion of Michigan—the Pigeon, Au Sable, White, Muskegon, and Rogue rivers. The hatch appears as early as mid-August and lasts into September. Al Rockwood forms the thorax using a dubbing loop.

Evergreen Drake

Pattern type: Eastern green drake (*Ephemera guttulata*) dun
Submitted by: Evergreen Fly Fishing Company (Clarksburg, West Virginia)
Originated by: Franklin Oliverio
Tied by: Franklin Oliverio

Hook: Dry fly 2XL, #8-#10
Thread: Primrose yellow 6/0
Tail: 4 or 5 peccary fibers
Body: Pale greenish yellow fur or synthetic dubbing
Shellback: Segment of dark pheasant tail fibers
Ribbing: White thread, wide
Wings: Mallard flank dyed pale green
Hackle: Grizzly dyed pale green

Top view

Comments: The tail of peccary fibers aids in floating this extremely popular West Virginia pattern.

Gray Mayfly

Pattern type: Mayfly adult
Submitted by: Corey's Handtied Flies (Yarmouth, Nova Scotia)
Originated by: Corey Burke
Tied by: Corey Burke

Hook: Mustad 7948A, #12-#18
Thread: Black 8/0
Tail: 3 strands dark moose hair
Body: Black tying thread
Ribbing: Fine gold or silver wire
Hackle: Grizzly

Green Drake

Comments: To tie the fly, attached the quill body extension to the shank. Tie the hackle-stem tails over the body. Mount 8-10 bucktail hairs at the base of the body; wrap up to the tail, then back to the hook shank, and tie off. Wrap tying thread up the body extension, then back down. Mount the wing feathers back-to-back; lacquer and press feathers together. Trim to shape. Mount and wrap hackle.

Pattern type: Green drake dun
Submitted by: Theriault Flies (Patten, Maine)
Originated by: Alvin Theriault
Tied by: Alvin Theriault

Hook: Mustad 94833, #8
Thread: Black 6/0 prewaxed
Tail: 3 stripped grizzly hen hackles
Body: Porcupine quill wrapped with yellow bucktail, tied extended, lacquered
Ribbing: Black 6/0 prewaxed
Wings: Two mallard breast feathers dyed drake yellow, tied back-to-back, lacquered and trimmed to shape
Hackle: One olive and one grizzly

This pattern can be tied in a variety of colors and sizes to match various mayfly hatches. Theriault fishes three flies simultaneously.

Hanson's Drake

Front view

Pattern type: Mayfly dun
Submitted by: Dan's Fly Shop (Roscommon, Michigan)
Originated by: Ann Schwiegert
Tied by: Dan Rivard

Hook: Dry fly #8-#18; or 3XL to 4XL #8-#12
Thread: Black flat 3/0
Tail: 3-4 pheasant tail fibers, 3 to 4 times hook gap
Body: Mottled turkey herl, well marked
Wings: Blue dun hackle tips
Hackle: Brown

Hex Trude

Pattern type: *Hexagenia limbata* dun, giant adult stonefly
Submitted by: Steelhead Connection Custom Flies (North Muskegon, Michigan)
Originated by: Adaptation of traditional Trude pattern
Tied by: Jeffrey P. Bonin

Hook: Mustad 9671 or 9672, #6
Thread: Tan Danville 3/0 Monocord
Tail: 8-10 lighter colored moose mane fibers
Body: Pale yellow or tan poly yarn (strand is split lengthwise before tying)
Wing: White calf tail
Hackle: Grizzly and brown, mixed

Comments: "The Hex Trude," Jeffrey Bonin points out, "developed as a simple yet durable pattern that could easily be tied for my customers. It is my top Hex pattern, especially when spinner falls are either very light or very heavy. It is also fantastic when the Hex hatch is recently passed, but the fish are still looking up for this large food item. The fly floats well and is easily seen at dusk and beyond, when the Hex fishing occurs.

When fishing very heavy spinner falls, I will cast upstream, to the right or left of the trout, then twitch the fly into his window. This technique with the Hex Trude will many times elicit a strike when fishing a traditional spinner pattern fails. Numerous times, I have been able to coax large trout into striking this pattern long after all feeding activity has ceased."

Hexagenia Limbata

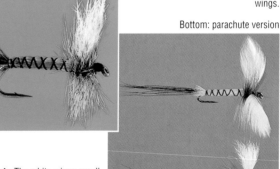

Top: version tied with white hackle-tip wings.

Bottom: parachute version

Pattern type: *Hexagenia limbata* dun
Submitted by: Backcast Fly Shop (Benzonia, Michigan)
Originated by: Backast Fly Shop
Tied by: John Kilmer

Hook: Mustad 94831, #4-#8
Thread: Black or brown
Tail: Moose mane
Body: Natural deer hair on top; golden yellow deer hair on underside
Ribbing: Black or brown tying thread
Wings: White calf tail (white hen-hackle tips for alternate version)
Hackle: Grizzly, brown, or both

Comments: The white wings on all versions of this pattern make the fly more visible, particularly in the evening when larger fish rise to the hex hatch.

Hi Vis Parachute Trico

Pattern type: Trico dun
Submitted by: The Superior Fly Angler (Superior, Wisconsin)
Originated by: Matt Paulson
Tied by: Matt Paulson

Hook: TMC 101, #20-#24
Thread: Black 8/0
Tail: Grizzly hackle fibers or Micro Fibetts
Body: Black Superfine dubbing
Wing: Orange poly yarn
Hackle: Grizzly

Comments: This is a good, high-visibility pattern designed for the faster riffles and runs of the upper Brule River.

Isonychia Cripple

Front view

Pattern type: Crippled *Isonychia* dun
Submitted by: Choo Choo Fly & Tackle (Chattanooga, Tennessee)
Originated by: Ryan Meulemans
Tied by: Ryan Meulemans

Hook: TMC 2487, #10
Thread: Brown 6/0
Tail: Rust Antron yarn
Body: Rust beaver dubbing
Collar: Butts of wing hair, clipped
Wing: Natural deer hair
Hackle: Grizzly, trimmed on bottom

Comments: "This fly," Ryan Meulemans notes, "was designed for the Hiwassee River in Tennessee. It floats well in broken water and supports a bead-head nymph very well for a dry-fly/dropper rig." Note that the hackle is wrapped between the clipped wing butts and the upright wings.

Jeff's Para Drake

Pattern type: Gray drake (*Siphlonurus alternatus, quebecensis, rapidus*) dun or spinner
Submitted by: Steelhead Connection Custom Flies (North Muskegon, Michigan)
Originated by: Version of standard parachute dun
Tied by: Jeffrey P. Bonin

Hook: Mustad 94840, #10-#14
Thread: Black or gray Dunville Flymaster 6/0
Tail: 6-8 moose mane fibers
Body: Fly-Rite #27 Speckled Dun/Light Hendrickson dubbing
Ribbing: Brown 3/0 Monocord
Wing: Gray Antron carpet fibers
Hackle: Medium dun

Comments: This fly represents either a dun or a spinner. The gray drake spinner, Jeffrey Bonin points out, frequently doesn't fall spent in the classic "spread eagle" position, but rather lands in odd positions, which may be better represented by this fly style. This prolific hatch provides some of the best fishing on Michigan's Muskegon River.

K & K Green Drake

Front view

Pattern type: Green drake dun
Submitted by: Mountain Valley Flies (Solon, Maine)
Originated by: John Kenealy
Tied by: John Kenealy

Hook: Mustad 94840 or Mustad 94832, #4-#14
Thread: Olive 6/0
Tail: Woodchuck guard hairs
Body: Yellowish-olive beaver dubbing
Wings: Woodchuck guard hairs
Hackle: Grizzly dyed olive and medium dun, mixed

Comments: "I developed this fly a few years ago," notes John Kenealy, "to imitate the large mayfly drakes on Maine trout ponds and also the Eastern green drakes. It can also be used as an attractor in the same way as the Wulff patterns."

Kenny's Invaria

Front view

Pattern type: Mayfly dun (*Ephemerella invaria*)
Submitted by: Delaware River Anglers (Willow Grove, Pennsylvania)
Originated by: Ken Schwam
Tied by: Ken Schwam

Hook: Mustad 94840, #14
Thread: Orange 6/0 Danville
Tail: Barred ginger and pale grizzly, mixed
Body: Light ginger hackle quill over orange thread
Wings: Wood duck
Hackle: Barred ginger and pale grizzly, mixed

Comments: Tyer Ken Schwam notes that this fly is particularly effective during the *Ephemerella invaria* hatches on the upper Delaware River and Catskill streams. It is also an effective attractor pattern.

Laur's Cat-dis–Brown Drake

Top view

Pattern type: Brown drake dun (or gray drake or mahogany dun)
Submitted by: Dan's Fly Shop (Roscommon, Michigan)
Originated by: Jerry Laur and Dan Rivard
Tied by: Jerry Laur

Hook: Dry-fly standard or 2XL, #8-#12
Thread: Yellow (or red or dark brown) flat 3/0
Tail: Moose hair from extended body
Egg sack: Yellow acrylic yarn
Body: Moose body hair
Ribbing: Tying thread
Wings: Chestnut mallard breast, hen or drake
Hackle: Brown (or brown and grizzly mixed)

Laur's Cat-dis–June Drake

Top view

Pattern type: *Hexagenia* dun or spinner
Submitted by: Dan's Fly Shop (Roscommon, Michigan)
Originated by: Jerry Laur
Tied by: Jerry Laur

Hook: 4XL, #4-#8
Thread: Yellow flat 3/0
Tail: Moose mane from body, trimmed to 3-5 fibers
Body: Moose mane, tied extended 4-8 segments beyond hook bend
Ribbing: Tying thread
Wings: Grizzly hen hackle tips or mallard flank feathers (hen or drake)
Hackle: Grizzly (brown, badger, furnace, or cree can also be used)

NB-Olive (No Brainer)

Front view

Pattern type: Blue-winged olive dun, green drake, March brown, or Dark Cahill dun
Submitted by: Park Place Exxon (Richwood, West Virginia)
Originated by: Oak Myers
Tied by: Oak Myers

Hook: TMC 100, #12-#18
Thread: Olive 6/0 Flymaster
Tail: Moose mane
Body: Olive Antron yarn
Wings: Spirit River Pre-cut Mayfly wings, #16-#18, medium olive
Hackle: Ginger

Comments: This fly, notes Oak Myers, is a highly productive pattern during a variety of mayfly hatches and holds its own with more specific "match-the-hatch" patterns. It is generally quite durable if a bit of care is taken with the wings.

Nemesis Parachute

Pattern type: Mayfly dun
Submitted by: The Sporting Gentleman (Media, Pennsylvania)
Originated by: Tom Fink
Tied by: Tom Fink

Hook: TMC 900BL, #16
Thread: Gray/dun Benecchi 12/0
Tail: 4 black deer or elk hairs
Abdomen: Grizzly hackle stem
Wing: Yearling elk hair
Thorax: Gray Kreinik silk dubbing
Hackle: Grizzly, tied off and whip-finished at base of wingpost beneath hackle wraps

Comments: This very effective dun imitation is best fished on flat water. The hackle is clipped away from the hook-eye area to facilitate threading the leader.

N.S. Mayfly

Top view

Pattern type:	Mayfly dun
Submitted by:	Corey's Handtied Flies (Yarmouth, Nova Scotia)
Originated by:	Corey Burke
Tied by:	Corey Burke
Hook:	Mustad 94840, #12-#14
Thread:	Black 8/0
Tail:	Black hackle fibers
Body:	Black tying thread
Wings:	Blue dun hen hackle tips
Hackle:	Black
Antennae (opt.):	Stripped black hackle stems

Comments: Corey Burke says, "This is one of the most widely accepted mayfly patterns in Nova Scotia. It is very successful with or without the antennae."

Para Poly Isonychia

Top view

Pattern type:	*Isonychia* dun
Submitted by:	The Fish Hawk (Atlanta, Georgia)
Originated by:	Robert Rooks, Jr.
Tied by:	Robert Rooks, Jr.
Hook:	TMC 100, #12
Thread:	Camel UNI 8/0
Tail:	Medium dun hackle fibers, tied long
Body:	Gray turkey quill
Ribbing:	Small copper wire, counterwrapped
Wing:	Gray poly yarn
Thorax:	Rusty Nature's Spirit Dubbing
Hackle:	Medium dun

Parachute Brown Drake

Pattern type:	Brown drake dun
Submitted by:	The Superior Fly Angler (Superior, Wisconsin)
Originated by:	Matt Paulson
Tied by:	Matt Paulson
Hook:	Mustad 94831, #10-#12
Thread:	Tan 6/0
Egg sac:	Yellow Superfine dubbing
Tail:	Micro Fibetts, tied split
Body:	Tan Superfine dubbing, mottled on top with brown Pantone marker
Wing:	White or light dun poly yarn, mottled with marker
Hackle:	Grizzly

Comments: This is a good brown drake pattern for faster sections of Wisconsin's Brule River that are in proximity to the slower, silty-bottomed areas that brown drake nymphs prefer.

Red Tree Rat

Front view

Pattern type:	Adult mayfly
Submitted by:	Severn Wharf Custom Rods (Gloucester Point, Virginia)
Originated by:	Richard Hines
Tied by:	Richard Hines
Hook:	Dry fly, #12-#18
Thread:	Brown 12/0
Tail:	Red fox squirrel tail
Body:	Natural Blend squirrel belly dubbing
Wings:	Red fox squirrel
Hackle:	Brown

Comments: Tyer Richard Hines says, "The Red Tree Rat imitates a light tan mayfly that is numerous in the waters of Shenandoah National Park. The natural is a size 12, but the brook trout seem to like this pattern best in sizes 14 to 18. It floats well in fast water and is easy to see. It works well on brooks and rainbows, and I've used it on the Rose, Rapidan, and Hughes rivers."

Roberts Yellow May

Pattern type: Yellow mayfly dun
Submitted by: Dan's Fly Shop (Roscommon, Michigan)
Originated by: Clarence Roberts
Tied by: Dan Rivard

Hook: Dry fly, #10-#16
Thread: Any light-colored flat 3/0
Tail: 3-4 strands pheasant tail fibers, 2 1/2 to 3 times hook gap
Body: Yellow floss
Wing: White deer hair
Hackle: Ginger

Skaneateles Brown Drake Comparadun

Pattern type: Brown drake adult
Submitted by: The Serious Angler (Jordan, New York)
Originated by: Steve Napoli version of Al Caucci design
Tied by: Steve Napoli

Hook: Mustad 94833, #10
Thread: Dark brown Danville 6/0
Tail: Brown Micro Fibetts
Body: Rusty spinner dubbing with a tinge of yellow mixed in
Wings: Coast deer hair, medium texture, dyed dun

Front view

Comments: Tyer Steve Napoli notes, "The brown drake natural on New York's Skaneateles Lake is much darker than those found on many rivers and streams. The bodies are a dark rusty brown with yellow segments, and the wings are a dark mottled gray, almost black. This fly is best fished when adult duns are present."

Tobin's March Brown

Pattern type: March brown dun
Submitted by: Beaverkill Angler (Roscoe, New York)
Originated by: Bill Tobin
Tied by: David E. Pabst

Hook: Mustad 94840, #10-#12
Thread: Orange 6/0
Tail: Bronze mallard
Body: Variegated (brown/white) wool
Wings: Bronze mallard
Hackle: Brown and grizzly mixed

Front view

Trico Dun

Pattern type: Trico dun and spinner
Submitted by: Nestor's Sporting Goods, Inc. (Quakertown and Whitehall, Pennsylvania)
Originated by: unknown
Tied by: Kenneth W. Mead

Hook: Wide-gap dry fly, #20-#26
Thread: Black (white for female version)
Tail: 2 Micro Fibbets, widely split, 1 1/2 to 2 times shank length
Abdomen: Black tying thread (white thread for female version)
Thorax: Black Superfine dubbing
Hackle: Grizzly, 2 turns over thorax; hackle should be 1 1/2 to 2 times hook gap

Top view of female version

Comments: Tyer Kenneth Mead notes that this pattern is usually fished as a dun but can be used as a spinner by clipping a deep "V" in the hackle on the underside of the body. This pattern is his version of a Trico dun he saw in Barry Beck's old fly shop.

Spinners

Adams–Spent Wing Parachute

Pattern type: Mayfly spinner
Submitted by: The Angler's Room
(Latrobe, Pennsylvania)
Originated by: Richard Rohrbaugh
Tied by: Richard Rohrbaugh

Hook: Dry fly, #16
Thread: Black
Tail: Cree hackle fibers
Body: Gray dubbing
Post: White poly yarn
Hackle: Cree
Wings: Grizzly hen saddle, burned to shape

Comments: To dress the fly, tie in the post. Tie in the wings adjacent to the post, one at a time. Mount the tail and dub the body to the post. Mount and wrap hackle; tie off. Pull wings back to dub in front of post, then wrap head and whip-finish.

Bent-Bodied Spinner
(Siphlonurus)

Top view

Side view

Pattern type: *Siphlonurus* spinner
Submitted by: North Country Angler
(Intervale, New Hampshire)
Originated by: Bill Thompson
Tied by: Bill Thompson

Hook: TMC 400T or Mustad 80150BR,
#12-#14
Thread: Dark brown 8/0
Tail: Micro Fibetts
Body: Rusty brown rabbit fur dubbing
Wings: Zing wing material burned or cut to shape
(wingpost of fluorescent yarn for parachute version)
Hackle: Blue dun, clipped on bottom

Comments: "This fly," says Bill Thompson, "is tied to fish the *Siphlonurus* spinner falls on the Saco River in North Conway, New Hampshire. The swimming nymph hook is used to give the impression of the twisted, bent shape of the spent spinners. Because spinner patterns are so difficult to see, I also tie the fly as a parachute pattern with a fluorescent yarn post."

Parachute version

Bent-Bodied Spinner (Siphlonurus mirus)

Top view

Side view

Pattern type: *Siphlonurus mirus* spinner
Submitted by: North Country Angler
(Intervale, New Hampshire)
Originated by: Bill Thompson
Tied by: Bill Thompson

Hook: TMC 400T or Mustad 80150BR,
#12
Thread: Yellow
Tail: Micro Fibetts
Body: Yellow fur dubbing; top markings added with brown Pantone pen
Wings: Zing wing material burned or cut to shape
Hackle: Coachman brown, clipped flat on bottom

Comments: Like Bill Thompson's *Siphlonurus* spinner, this version is tied for the Saco River. "The *mirus* spinners," he explains, "will often fall at the same time as the *Siphlonurus*. The trout will key in on the yellow-bodied spinners and leave the more abundant brown ones alone. The *mirus* has a very distinct chocolate-brown secondary wing, represented by the coachman brown hackle."

Bob's Trico Spinner

Pattern type:	Trico spinner
Submitted by:	Oak Orchard Fly Shop (Williamsville, New York)
Originated by:	Bob Morrissey
Tied by:	Bob Morrissey
Hook:	TMC 101, #26
Thread:	White UNI 8/0 and black UNI 14/0
Tail:	White Micro Fibetts
Abdomen:	White tying thread
Wings:	Zing wing material
Thorax:	Black tying thread
Legs:	Black Chinese boar fibers

CDC Egg Laying Spinner
(Hendrickson)

Front view

Pattern type:	Egg-laying Hendrickson spinner (*Ephemerella subvaria*)
Submitted by:	Tulpehocken Creek Outfitters (Reading, Pennsylvania)
Originated by:	Tony Gehman and Dave Eshenower
Tied by:	Tony Gehman and Dave Eshenower
Hook:	TMC 100, #12-#16
Thread:	Rusty dun UNI 8/0
Tail:	Dun Micro Fibetts
Egg sac:	Sulphur yellow TCO East Coast Dubbing
Body:	Hendrickson red quill TCO East Coast Dubbing
Wings:	TCO natural CDC

Comments: "This pattern," observe Tony Gehman and Dave Eshenower, "is best fished in the first or last hour of the day when trout are keying on spent spinners. This egg-sac version drives trout crazy. We tie the CDC in an upright fashion, making it more visible to the angler."

Coleman's Hendrickson Spinner Oatka

Front view

Pattern type:	Hendrickson spinner
Submitted by:	Coleman's Fly Shop (Spencerport, New York)
Originated by:	Carl Coleman
Tied by:	Carl Coleman
Hook:	Daiichi 1180, #14
Thread:	Red UNI 8/0
Tail:	3 or 4 light dun Micro Fibetts, twice body length
Ribbing:	Brown 4X Maxima tippet material, or clear mono tinted brown with marker
Body:	Mad River Dubbing #40
Hackle:	6 or 7 wraps light blue dun Metz neck or saddle, twice hook gap, clipped on bottom

Comments: Carl Coleman advises keeping the body on this pattern sparse. The clipped hackle wing makes this fly visible to the angler and does not twist the leader during casting as other spinner patterns can.

Coleman's Male Sulfur

Front view

Pattern type:	Sulphur spinner
Submitted by:	Coleman's Fly Shop (Spencerport, New York)
Originated by:	Carl Coleman
Tied by:	Carl Coleman
Hook:	Daiichi 1180, #16
Thread:	Fire orange UNI 8/0
Tail:	3-4 light dun Micro Fibetts, twice shank length
Tag:	Fire orange tying thread, 1/32" beyond tip of abdomen
Body:	2 layers of fire orange tying thread
Ribbing:	Stripped dark dun hackle stem
Hackle:	5-6 wraps Metz light blue dun, twice hook gap, clipped on bottom

Comments: After tying the body and ribbing, coat with vinyl cement for durabilty.

Coleman's Sulfur Spinner Female

Pattern type: Sulphur spinner
Submitted by: Coleman's Fly Shop (Spencerport, New York)
Originated by: Carl Coleman
Tied by: Carl Coleman

Hook: Daiichi 1180, #16
Thread: Yellow UNI 8/0
Tail: Light dun Micro Fibetts, twice shank length
Body: 3 layers of yellow tying thread
Ribbing: Stripped cream hackle stem
Indicator: Chartreuse Glo-Bug yarn, 1/8" to 3/16" long
Hackle: Light blue dun, 4-6 turns, clipped on bottom

Comments: After tying the body and ribbing, coat them with vinyl cement for durability. The indicator yarn on this pattern makes it easy to see.

Evergreen Coffin Fly

Pattern type: Eastern green drake (*Ephemera guttulata*) spinner
Submitted by: Evergreen Fly Fishing Company (Clarksburg, West Virginia)
Originated by: Franklin Oliverio
Tied by: Franklin Oliverio

Hook: Dry fly 2XL, #8-#10
Thread: White 6/0
Tail: 4 or 5 peccary fibers
Body: White closed-cell foam
Ribbing: White thread
Wings: Mallard flank feather
Hackle: Silver badger

Comments: This pattern can be fished dead drift or skittered across the surface. The white thread ribbing is used to segment the foam body.

Invaria Para

Pattern type: *Ephemerella invaria* spinner
Submitted by: North Country Angler (Intervale, New Hampshire)
Originated by: Bill Thompson
Tied by: Bill Thompson

Hook: Dry fly, #14
Thread: Brown 8/0
Tail: Blue dun hackle fibers
Body: Rust brown goose biot
Wing: White turkey flat
Hackle: Blue dun

Comments: Tied for the *invaria* spinner fall on New Hampshire's Saco River, this pattern floats low but has a white wing for good visibility.

Jay's Brown Drake Spinner

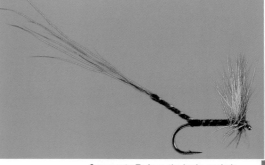

Pattern type: Brown drake spinner
Submitted by: Coleman's Fly Shop (Spencerport, New York)
Originated by: Jay Peck
Tied by: Jay Peck

Hook: Daiichi 1180, #8
Thread: Brown UNI 8/0
Tail: Tips of hair from extended body
Body: 12-15 strands medium brown bucktail, 4 times shank length
Ribbing: Fine yellow floss
Hackle: 6 wraps light blue dun, followed by 3 wraps medium brown; clipped on bottom

Comments: To form the body, encircle yellow floss with bucktail fiber and attach to shank. Wrap back beyond hook bend, spiraling thread around bucktail to form extended body. When base of tail is reached, spiral thread back to shank. Clip off half the fibers at the base of tail, leaving other half to form the tails. Spiral yellow floss forward to form ribbing.

Jay's Green Drake Spinner

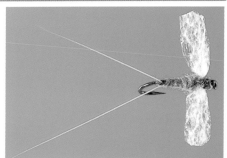

Front view

Pattern type:	Green drake spinner
Submitted by:	Coleman's Fly Shop (Spencerport, New York)
Originated by:	Jay Peck
Tied by:	Jay Peck
Hook:	Daiichi 1180, #8
Thread:	White UNI 8/0
Tail:	6-10 medium stiff black bear hairs
Body:	8-10 white bucktail fibers encircling tailing fibers; tie extended by spiraling thread up to tail base, then back to shank
Wings:	Teal flank
Hackle:	2 silver badger hackles, clipped on bottom

Jon's Bubble Wing Spinner

Pattern type:	Mayfly spinner
Submitted by:	North Country Angler (Intervale, New Hampshire)
Originated by:	Jon Howe
Tied by:	Jon Howe
Hook:	Dry fly, #12-#18
Thread:	Brown
Tail:	White or dun Micro Fibetts
Body:	Light brown Superfine dubbing
Wings:	Thin, closed-cell packing foam (Ethafoam)

Comments: The foam wings give good buoyancy to this low-floating pattern, which is tied for the many spinner falls on New Hampshire's Saco River.

Kid's Loop Wing Spinner

Comments: The wings on this fly are made from saddle hackle with barbs slightly longer than the finished wingspan of the fly. Tyer John Harter prefers a soft-stemmed type of hackle such as Hoffman. The wings are mounted at or near the center of the shank. Tie in the trimmed stem (by the tip) atop the shank with the stem angled to the rear on the far side of the hook. Form the far wing by bringing the stem forward, past the eye, and angling it to the rear of the hook on the near side of the shank. Secure the wing with 3 crisscross wraps. Reverse the loop process to form the near wing. The loops should be slightly larger than the hook gap.

Pattern type:	Blue-winged olive spinner
Submitted by:	Morning Dew Anglers (Berwick, Pennsylvania)
Originated by:	John Harter
Tied by:	John Harter
Hook:	TMC 100, #14-#16
Thread:	Gray 8/0 (or color to match body for alternate versions)
Tail:	Moose hair or clear Micro Fibetts, 3 fibers each side
Body:	Olive dubbing (or colors to match other naturals)
Wings:	Saddle hackle, trimmed close to stem
Hackle:	Dun (or to match natural, e.g., cream for sulphur spinners, grizzly for March brown, etc.), clipped even with hook point on bottom

Simple Hex Spinner

Comments: This fly is easy and quick to tie, "so you don't have to feel too bad when you hang one in a tree at midnight," says tyer Mark Lord.

Pattern type:	*Hexagenia limbata* spinner
Submitted by:	Streamside Orvis (Williamsburg, Michigan)
Originated by:	Mark Lord
Tied by:	Mark Lord
Hook:	Orvis 1526, #4-#6
Thread:	Yellow 6/0
Tail:	2 stripped grizzly hackle stems or 2 strands peccary hair
Underbody:	Yellow yarn
Overbody:	Natural deer hair, tips tied in and flared at rear, pulled over top of yarn and crisscrossed with tying thread
Wings:	White poly yarn (or deer hair or Z-lon)
Hackle:	Brown and grizzly mixed (or cree or barred ginger)

Side view

Skaneateles Brown Drake Spinner

Top view

Pattern type: Brown drake spinner
Submitted by: The Serious Angler (Jordan, New York)
Originated by: Steve Napoli
Tied by: Steve Napoli

Hook: Mustad 94833, #10
Thread: Dark brown Danville 6/0
Tail: Brown Micro Fibetts
Body: Rust spinner dubbing with a tinge of yellow mixed in
Wings: Coastal deer hair, medium texture, dyed dun

Comments: This pattern, tied for New York's Skaneateles Lake, is best fished to cruising fish, says Steve Napoli, by landing the fly just ahead of the fish and twitching it a tiny bit to represent a struggling or dying natural.

TCO Sparkle Wing Spinner
(Trico)

Top view

Pattern type: Trico spinner
Submitted by: Tulpehocken Creek Outfitters (Reading, Pennsylvania)
Originated by: Tony Gehman and Dave Eshenower
Tied by: Tony Gehman and Dave Eshenower

Hook: TMC 2488, #20-#26
Thread: White UNI 17/0
Tail: Dun Micro Fibetts
Abdomen: White tying thread
Wings: White Darlon
Thorax: Trico spinner TCO East Coast Dubbing

Comments: The extra-wide gap on the hook style used here helps keep hooking percentages high on the very small hooks used for Trico imitations.

CHAPTER **3**

Caddisflies

Larvae

Bead Head/Bead Bodied Caddis

Red version

Pattern type:	Caddis larva
Submitted by:	Housatonic River Outfitters, Inc. (West Cornwall, Connecticut)
Originated by:	Harold McMillan
Tied by:	Harold McMillan

Hook:	Daiichi 1150, #10-#18
Thread:	Olive Danville 6/0
Tail:	Blend of olive synthetic dubbing and chartreuse rabbit fur
Abdomen:	3 green bi-colored beads (red for red version, or any color to match natural)
Thorax:	Blend of olive synthetic dubbing and chartreuse rabbit fur
Head:	1/8" tungsten bead

Comments: "This caddis larva pattern," notes Harold McMillan, "is an extremely accurate imitation of various caddis larvae here in the East. It is as effective as it is simple. When caddis are active in a river, it will catch fish by the score." The bi-colored beads in this pattern are clear beads with a colored core.

Candy Cane Caddis

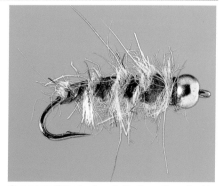

Pattern type:	Cased caddis
Submitted by:	The Sporting Tradition (Lexington, Kentucky)
Originated by:	Rick Fowler
Tied by:	Rob Fightmaster

Hook:	TMC 200R, #12-#16
Thread:	Olive 6/0
Body:	Natural hare's ear dubbing
Ribbing:	Olive Scud Back
Head:	Gold metal bead

Comments: This simple and effective pattern should be fished dead drift wherever caddis are present.

C.K. Nymph

Pattern type: Cased caddis
Submitted by: The Fish Hawk (Atlanta, Georgia)
Originated by: Chuck Kraft
Tied by: Henry Williamson

Hook: TMC 3761, #12-#16; weighted with .010" lead wire
Thread: Black UNI 8/0
Tail: Wood duck flank fibers, tied short and thick
Body: Black dubbing
Hackle: Grizzly saddle, palmered and trimmed to taper toward rear of fly

Comments: Henry Williamson explains, "This pattern is an everyday, meat-and-potatoes fly for this corner of the world—western North Carolina and South Carolina, north Georgia, and east Tennessee. It is fished dead drift with a split shot and/or strike indicator, and sometimes dropped underneath a dry fly. Fly fisher folks in the Altanta area sometimes call this same fly the 'Anytime Anywhere.'"

Cocky Knight

Pattern type: Cased caddis
Submitted by: Drury's Buffalo Valley Outfitters (Natrona Heights, Pennsylvania)
Originated by: unknown
Tied by: Rick Drury

Hook: Mustad 79580, #6-#10
Thread: Black 6/0
Tail: Pheasant tail fibers
Body: Gray/brown rabbit dubbing
Ribbing: Grizzly hackle, clipped short (brown hackle for alternate version)

Version with brown hackle rib

Comments: Says tyer Rick Drury, "The Cocky Knight is a regional pattern popular in western Pennsylvania for the last half-century. Little known in the retail business and seldom sold, it has been kept alive by private tyers in the area. The origins of the pattern are long lost, but it is plainly an attempt to imitate the cased caddis so abundant in local waters. Fished in the typical nymph fashion, the fly has a buggy appearance that appeals to trout everywhere."

Coulee Caddis

Pattern type: Caddis larva
Submitted by: Fly and Field (Glen Ellyn, Illinois)
Originated by: Daniel Grant
Tied by: Daniel Grant

Hook: TMC 2457, #8-#18; weighted with .020" lead wire
Thread: Black 6/0
Tail: Hare's mask
Underbody: Fluorescent green Glo-Bright Superfloss
Overbody: Chartreuse Vinyl Rib, medium
Legs: Black hare's ear dubbing
Head: Black metal bead

Comments: "This fly," notes tyer Daniel Grant, "was designed for the coulee region of southwest Wisconsin. It is mostly fished dead drift in a tandem-fly rig, but it is also very effective using a hand-twist retrieve."

Hester's Little Green Rock Worm

Pattern type: Caddis larva
Submitted by: Chesapeake Fly & Bait Company (Arnold, Maryland)
Originated by: Jim Hester
Tied by: Jim Hester

Hook: Nymph, #12-#14; weight, optional
Thread: Black Danville Flymaster 6/0
Body: Chartreuse Lumi-Flex or UNI-Stretch
Legs: 1 to 1 1/2 wraps pearlescent black Micro Cactus Chenille

Comments: Jim Hester notes, "The 'Green Weenie' patterns are very popular in Maryland and south-central Pennsylvania. This pattern is very effective at the Gunpowder River and Deer Creek in Maryland, as well as other local streams."

Hydro

Pattern type: Caddis larva
Submitted by: Wilderness Trekker (Orwigsburg, Pennsylvania)
Originated by: Todd R. Seigfried
Tied by: Todd R. Seigfried

Hook: Caddis pupa, #10-#16; weighted with .016" lead on front 1/3 of shank
Thread: Gray 8/0
Tail: Tuft of gray marabou
Body: Pale brownish-gray Scintilla (#37) dubbing
Ribbing: 4x monofilament tippet material
Legs: Dark brown partridge feather
Shellback: Latex strip; last 2 head segments colored black with Pantone marker, rest of shellback colored with brown Pantone marker

Comments: The legs on this patterns are formed by mounting a partridge feather at the midpoint of the shank. After completing the body, draw the feather forward over the top of the thorax and tie off. Clip the feather barbs to length. The shellback material is drawn forward over the top of the legs. Tyer Todd Seigfried notes that this pattern is based on concepts taken from Roy Beckmeyer, Oliver Edwards, and Vit Misar.

Rube's Woven Caddis

Pattern type: Caddis larva
Submitted by: Housatonic River Outfitters, Inc. (West Cornwall, Connecticut)
Originated by: Don Rubenstein
Tied by: Don Rubenstein

Hook: Shrimp hook, #8; weighted with lead wire which is covered with tying thread
Thread: Black Monocord
Body: Black and chartreuse Antron, woven with Pott's Weave
Rib: Pearl thread
Legs: Gray CDC

Comments: Don Rubenstein explains, "I wet the CDC with saliva and fish this deep. This gives plenty of action to the legs. I also fish this as an emerger by applying Frog Fanny to just the CDC. This makes the CDC carry an air bubble that is so lifelike that the fish cannot resist."

Simple Green

Pattern type: *Rhyacophila* caddis larva
Submitted by: The Fish Hawk (Atlanta, Georgia)
Originated by: unknown
Tied by: Robert Rooks, Jr.

Hook: TMC 200R, #14-#18
Thread: Black UNI 8/0
Body: Caddis green Nature's Spirit Dubbing
Gills: Small natural ostrich herl, one strand along each side, pulled forward and secured with ribbing
Ribbing: Small copper wire
Head: Black ostrich herl

The Fly

Pattern type: Caddis larva of Hydropsychidae and Rhyacophilidae families
Submitted by: Thornapple Orvis Shop (Grand Rapids, Michigan)
Originated by: Dave Hise
Tied by: Dave Hise

Hook: TMC 206BL or scud/caddis hook, #10-#18
Thread: Olive UNI 8/0
Abdomen: Insect green Flex-Floss segmented with caddis green Krystal Dub
Ribbing: Fine copper wire
Thorax: Medium brown Krystal Dub, picked out and trimmed on top

Comments: "This pattern," notes Dave Hise, "is extremely productive throughout the year on many of the rivers and streams of lower Michigan, especially the Muskegon, Rogue, and Pere Marquette. It's great for trout and steelhead and also effective on some of the major tailwaters of the West."

Waydowner

Pattern type:	Caddis larva
Submitted by:	Maine Sport Outfitters (Rockport, Maine)
Originated by:	Terry Walsh
Tied by:	Terry Walsh

Hook:	TMC 2487, #10-#16
Thread:	Black 6/0
Abdomen:	Bright green Antron body wool, twisted into tight rope, blackened on top with waterproof marker
Ribbing:	Fine silver oval tinsel
Thorax:	Peacock herl
Legs:	Olive pheasant tail fibers
Head:	Tungsten bead

Comments: The tungsten bead sinks this fly quickly to get deep in Maine's fast-moving rivers. Tyer Terry Walsh fishes it in tandem with a Pheasant Tail or other nymph pattern.

Pupae

Antron Winged Caddis Pupa

Pattern type:	Caddis pupa
Submitted by:	Great Lakes Fly Fishing Company (Rockford, Michigan)
Originated by:	Bob Braendle
Tied by:	Ben Hunting

Hook:	TMC 200R, #16-#20
Thread:	Brown or color to match natural
Body:	Green hare's ear or hare's ear/Antron blend, or color to match natural
Wings:	Dark brown Darlon, Antron, or Z-lon tied in 1/4 from rear, pulled forward and tied off at head/body junction
Legs:	Partridge or hen fibers tied beard style
Eyes:	Hareline Nymph Eyes
Head:	Dark brown hare's ear or hare's ear/Antron blend, or color to match natural

Brett's Light Scud Back Caddis

Top view

Pattern type:	Caddis pupa
Submitted by:	Coleman's Fly Shop (Spencerport, New York)
Originated by:	Brett Jackson
Tied by:	Brett Jackson

Hook:	Daiichi 1150, #14-#16
Thread:	Yellow UNI 8/0
Abdomen:	Clear Scud Back over yellow thread underbody
Ribbing:	Gold wire
Wings:	White goose biot
Thorax:	Gray ostrich herl
Head:	Gold metal bead

Brett's Scud Back Caddis

Pattern type: Caddis pupa
Submitted by: Coleman's Fly Shop (Spencerport, New York)
Originated by: Brett Jackson
Tied by: Brett Jackson

Hook: Daiichi 1150, #14-#16
Thread: Olive UNI 8/0
Abdomen: Olive Scud Back, wrapped
Ribbing: Medium copper wire
Wing: Light blue dun saddle hackle fibers
Thorax: Peacock herl
Head: Gold metal bead

Comments: Fish this pattern close to the bottom in riffles using a split shot about 10" above the fly and a strike indicator. At the end of each drift, let the fly swing up or twitch it slowly to the surface.

Green Caddis Pupa

Pattern type: Caddis pupa, general attractor
Submitted by: Backcast Fly Shop (Benzonia, Michigan)
Originated by: Mike Tyler
Tied by: Mike Tyler Flies

Hook: TMC 2457 or Mustad 80200R, #6-#10
Thread: Black
Abdomen: Bright green to olive yarn or dubbing
Thorax: Peacock herl
Legs: Natural bird body feathers—partridge, pheasant, turkey, etc.

Oatka Prince

Top view

Pattern type: Caddis pupa
Submitted by: Coleman's Fly Shop (Spencerport, New York)
Originated by: Brett Jackson
Tied by: Brett Jackson

Hook: Daiichi 1150, #14-#16
Thread: Rusty brown UNI 8/0
Abdomen: Tying thread built to taper toward rear
Ribbing: Gold wire
Wings: White goose biots
Thorax: Dyed yellow peacock herl
Head: Gold metal bead

Tinsel Caddis Pupa (Black)

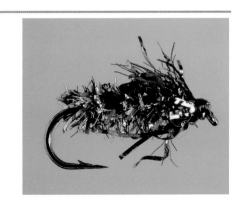

Pattern type: Black caddis pupa
Submitted by: Chesapeake Fly & Bait Company (Arnold, Maryland)
Originated by: Jim Hester
Tied by: Jim Hester

Hook: Wet fly or nymph, #10-#12
Thread: Black Danville Flymaster 6/0
Body: Danville Rainbow Crystal Chenille and pearlescent black Micro Cactus Chenille twisted together and wrapped, clipped
Legs: 1 /1/2 wraps pearlescent black Cactus Chenille

Emergers

Bob's Teardrop Caddis Emerger/Stillborn

Front view

Pattern type:	Caddis emerger, stillborn
Submitted by:	Great Lakes Fly Fishing Company (Rockford, Michigan)
Originated by:	Bob Braendle
Tied by:	Fred Vargas

Hook:	TMC 2487, #16-#20
Thread:	Dark brown or color to match natural
Body:	Tan Superfine dubbing or color to match natural
Shuck:	Amber Antron, Darlon, or Z-lon, pulled over body and gathered beyond hook bend with tying thread; excess is clipped then butts melted with heated dubbing needle or cauterizing tool
Hackle:	3-4 wraps of grizzly dyed green or brown, or color to match natural, clipped short on top and bottom
Wings:	Dun poly yarn (or deer hair or snowshoe rabbit)

Comments: Details about dressing this pattern can be found in *Caddis Super Hatches*, by Bob Braendle and Carl Richards.

B.T. Nymph

Pattern type:	Caddis emerger
Submitted by:	Dakota Angler & Outfitter (Rapid City, South Dakota)
Originated by:	Tyler Smoragiewicz
Tied by:	Tyler Smoragiewicz

Hook:	TMC 5262, #12-#16
Thread:	Black or olive Benecchi 12/0
Body:	Peacock herl
Hackle:	Hen hackle, black with gray/white tips

Comments: The "B.T." in this pattern stands for "brook trout."

CDC Pop Caddis
(Emerald Green)

Yellow Tan version

Pattern type:	Caddis emerger
Submitted by:	Tulpehocken Creek Outfitters (Reading, Pennsylvania)
Originated by:	Tony Gehman and Dave Eshenower
Tied by:	Tony Gehman and Dave Eshenower

Hook:	TMC 2487, #14-#22
Thread:	Rusty Dun UNI 8/0
Abdomen:	Emerald green TCO East Coast Dubbing (yellow tan dubbing for Yellow Tan version)
Thorax:	Caddis thorax blend TCO East Coast Dubbing
Wings:	TCO natural CDC
Legs:	Mottled hen back fibers

Comments: Tony Gehman and Dave Eshenower note, "This pattern will fool the most wary trout due to the fact that we tie the CDC facing forward, causing the fly to ride vertically in the surface film and wiggle because of the shape of the hook. Perfect for finicky trout sipping emerging caddis."

CDC Soft Hackle Caddis (Emerald Green)

Pattern type: Caddis emerger
Submitted by: Tulpehocken Creek Outfitters (Reading, Pennsylvania)
Originated by: Tony Gehman and Dave Eshenower
Tied by: Tony Gehman and Dave Eshenower

Hook: TMC 2487, #14-#18
Thread: Rusty Dun UNI 8/0
Abdomen: Emerald green TCO East Coast Dubbing
Underwing: Pearl Darlon
Wings: TCO natural CDC
Thorax: Peacock herl

Comments: Tony Gehman and Dave Eshenower explain, "This pattern was designed to flash and 'breathe' in the water as you swing it through the riffles. The addition of CDC makes the fly trail air bubles as it swims."

Jay's Blast Off Caddis

Top view

Pattern type: Caddis emerger
Submitted by: Coleman's Fly Shop (Spencerport, New York)
Originated by: Jay Peck
Tied by: Jay Peck

Hook: Daiichi 1150, #16
Thread: Olive UNI 8/0
Abdomen: Olive Antron dubbing
Ribbing: Fine silver wire
Wings: White Antron and 2 mallard quill segments
Thorax: Muskrat dubbing

Comments: Jay Peck advises, "Cast this fly close to the bank, and let it sink by mending the line a few times. Then slowly lift the rod tip."

Jay's Light Caddis Emerger

Pattern type: Caddis emerger
Submitted by: Coleman's Fly Shop (Spencerport, New York)
Originated by: Jay Peck
Tied by: Jay Peck

Hook: Daiichi 1180, #16
Thread: Yellow UNI 8/0
Body: Light olive Mad River #19 dubbing
Wings: Small clump of wood duck flank fibers and white Antron
Hackle: 3 turns brown partridge

Comments: This fly is fished down-and-across in the traditional wet-fly manner.

L.A.S. Emerger

Pattern type: Caddis emerger
Submitted by: Whitetop Laurel Fly Shop (West Jefferson, North Carolina)
Originated by: Lowell A. Shipe
Tied by: Lowell A. Shipe

Hook: Mustad 80250BR or 80200BR, #12-#18
Thread: Olive 6/0 pre-waxed
Tail: 4 strands moose mane
Body: Mixture of orange, olive, and yellow Hare-Tron dubbing
Wings: Light gray deer hair
Head: Peacock herl

Comments: This fly is tied for the creeks and streams of northwest North Carolina, southwest Virginia, and northeast Tennessee. "It's designed," says Lowell Shipe, "to float low in the film, with the body below the surface. This fly fishes best on a dead drift, then swung, and then skipped back to you."

Peacock Emerger

Pattern type:	Caddis emerger or pupa
Submitted by:	The Forks Fly Shop (Inglewood, Ontario)
Originated by:	Wayne F. Martin
Tied by:	Wayne F. Martin
Hook:	TMC 102Y, #16–#28
Thread:	Black
Tail:	3-4 dun rooster hackle fibers
Abdomen:	Peacock herl
Thorax:	Western olive Fly Rite #29 dubbing
Wing:	Snowshoe rabbit foot, folded into loop
Hackle:	2 turns dark ginger hen hackle

Comments: This fly can be fish dead drift or given a slight action with the rod tip in slower water.

Pheasant Tail Variant

Pattern type:	Caddis emerger
Submitted by:	Gloria Jordan's Fly Rod Shop (Manchester Center, Vermont)
Originated by:	Gloria Jordan
Tied by:	Gloria Jordan
Hook:	Mustad 94840, #14
Thread:	Black Danville waxed
Tail:	Dun Micro Fibetts
Body:	Pheasant tail fibers
Ribbing:	Fine gold wire
Hackle:	Oversize blue dun

Comments: "This fly," explains tyer Gloria Jordan, "has proven effective on the Battenkill and Mettawee rivers. I feel the gold wire helps to attract fish, and the fly skitters along on the surface, getting much attention. Fish it as a dry fly any time of day—casting upstream, mending line, and fishing it across and down. It's a fun pattern to use and easy to tie."

QD Caddis Emerger

Front view

Pattern type:	Caddis emerger/stillborn
Submitted by:	Great Lakes Fly Fishing Company (Rockford, Michigan)
Originated by:	Bob Braendle
Tied by:	Fred Vargas
Hook:	TMC 200R, #16–#20
Thread:	Olive or color to match natural
Shuck:	Amber Antron, Darlon, or Z-lon, or color to match natural; tied in at rear of hook and pulled forward over body
Body:	Green Superfine dubbing or color to match natural
Hackle:	3-4 wraps of grizzly dyed brown or olive or color to match natural; "V" clipped on bottom
Wings:	Gray poly yarn (or deer hair or snowshoe rabbit)

Red Arsed Olive Soft Hackle

Pattern type:	Caddis emerger
Submitted by:	The Fly Fisherman's Place (Thomaston, Maine)
Originated by:	Terry Walsh
Tied by:	Terry Walsh
Hook:	Daiichi 1130, #12–#18
Thread:	Olive 6/0
Tag:	Red dubbing
Body:	Olive rabbit fur dubbing with trace of rust rabbit
Ribbing:	Fine gold oval tinsel
Hackle:	2 turns brown soft hackle, 1/3 body length
Head:	2 turns of body dubbing

Scraggly

Pattern type: Caddis emerger, alderfly adult
Submitted by: Hair & Things Guide Service and
Fly Shop (Rutland, Vermont)
Originated by: Russ Ryder
Tied by: Paul R. Buccheri

Hook: TMC 5263, #14-#16
Thread: Black Monocord
Body: Peacock herl with grizzly hackle
palmered and clipped short
Ribbing: Gold wire
Hackle: Hen furnace, prepared as shown in
photo and tied in at butt end

Hackle feather prepared for the pattern. The feather is clipped to leave a 1/2" section of barbs on the stem, then the barbs on one side are trimmed to a length of 3/16".

Comments: Fished deep, this fly imitates a cased caddis; fished in the film, it makes a caddis emerger. Dressed with floatant and fished dry, it becomes an adult alderfly. The pattern was designed for early-June fishing on the Connecticut and Androscoggin rivers.

Sebago Caddis

Pattern type: Caddis emerger
Submitted by: Sebago Fly Shop (Steep Falls, Maine)
Originated by: Bob Thorne
Tied by: Bob Thorne

Hook: 2XL wet fly, #12
Thread: Black 3/0 Monocord
Tail: Golden pheasant tippet
Body: Peacock herl, 5 or 6 strands
Wings: Turkey quill dyed dark blue dun
Hackle: Brown, throat style

Comments: This pattern is tied for landlocked salmon and brown trout. It should be retrieved very slowly.

Stevens' Caddis Cripple

Pattern type: Tan caddis emerger or stillborn
Submitted by: The Sporting Gentleman of Delaware (Centreville, Delaware)
Originated by: Dawn Stevens
Tied by: Dawn Stevens

Hook: Scud, #16
Thread: Tan 8/0
Shuck: Brown/olive Antron
Body: Tan Squirrel Brite dubbing
Wings: Natural CDC, clipped
Hackle: 1 or 2 turns of ruffed or blue grouse
Head: Black opalescent glass bead

Comments: Tyer Dawn Stevens explains, "This fly imitates a #16 tan caddis found on many waters in the mid-Atlantic states. It is effective used as an emerger (fished on the swing) and a stillborn (fished dead drift, both sunken and in the film). It is also my pattern of choice when first fishing a stream—my searching pattern."

Tan Double Bubble

Pattern type: Caddis emerger
Submitted by: Wilderness Trekker
(Orwigsburg, Pennsylvania)
Originated by: Todd R. Seigfried
Tied by: Todd R. Seigfried

Hook: Caddis pupa, #12-#16
Thread: Dark brown 8/0
Body: 2 pearlescent plastic beads alternating
on shank with tan Antron dubbing
Legs: 2 turns of dark brown partridge
Bubble: Veil of tan Antron tied in behind head and
sweeping to hook bend
Head: Dark brown ostrich herl

Top view

Adults

Alderfly

Pattern type: Adult caddis
Submitted by: North Country Angler (Intervale, New Hampshire)
Originated by: Bill Thompson
Tied by: Bill Thompson

Hook: Dry fly, #12
Thread: Dark brown 8/0
Body: Gray muskrat dubbing
Ribbing: Medium blue dun hackle, palmered over body, clipped flat on top
Wings: Pheasant body feather, clipped to shape and coated with Dave's Flexament
Antennae: Stripped brown hackle quills

Top view

Comments: Bill Thompson notes, "The alderfly, or more accurately, the zebra caddis (*Macronema zebratum*), is a very important hatch on the Androscoggin River in New Hampshire. The hatch occurs about the last week of June and can produce some of the best dry-fly fishing of the year. This pattern was developed to give a more realistic representation of the alderfly. It is best in flat water where the trout have a little longer to look things over."

Black Diving Caddis

Pattern type: Diving caddis
Submitted by: Dan's Fly Shop (Roscommon, Michigan)
Originated by: Dan Rivard
Tied by: Dan Rivard

Hook: Wet fly, #12-#18
Thread: Black flat 3/0
Tail: Olive acrylic yarn, one hook gap in length
Body: Crow or blackbird body feather, wrapped
Ribbing (opt.): Fine silver wire
Wing: Black feather flanked by silver tinsel

Comments: Dan Rivard suggests fishing this pattern by putting a metal bead on the leader, tying on the fly, then sliding the bead down to the hook eye.

Canary Caddis

Pattern type: Adult caddis, general attractor
Submitted by: Adirondack Sport Shop (Wilmington, New York)
Originated by: Kevin Henebry
Tied by: Kevin Henebry

Hook: TMC 100, #12-#16
Thread: Cream or white 8/0 pre-waxed
Body: Pale yellow dubbing
Wing: Elk hair dyed yellow
Hackle: Ginger

Comments: The wing on this pattern is tied in 3 layers. A small amount of dubbing is applied at the rear of the hook, and then a small clump of elk hair is tied in ahead of the dubbing. The body is dubbing forward, then a second clump of elk hair is tied in so that the tips are aligned with those of the first clump. A third section of dubbing and another clump of elk hair are then added. The hackle is wrapped over the butts of the last clump of wing material.

Carpet Caddis

Pattern type: Adult caddis
Submitted by: Dakota Angler & Outfitter (Rapid City, South Dakota)
Originated by: Hans Stephenson
Tied by: Hans Stephenson

Hook: Partridge E1A Hooper series, #14-#18
Thread: Brown 10/0
Body: Brown Carpet Twist, burned at rear
Legs: Brown CDC
Wing: Coarse deer hair

Comments: The legs are formed by twisting CDC onto the thread, like dubbing; the longer fibers will project out to form legs.

CDC Adult Caddis (Emerald Green)

Pattern type: Adult caddis
Submitted by: Tulpehocken Creek Outfitters (Reading, Pennsylvania)
Originated by: Tony Gehman and Dave Eshenower
Tied by: Tony Gehman and Dave Eshenower

Hook: TMC 2487, #14-#22
Thread: Rusty dun UNI 8/0
Abdomen: Emerald green TCO East Coast Dubbing
Wings: TCO natural CDC
Thorax: Caddis thorax blend TCO East Coast Dubbing

Comments: Tony Gehman and Dave Eshenower observe, "This pattern is designed to float very well due to the amount of CDC and the method used to prepare it. We don't use the feather tips. Instead, we strip the fibers from the stems of 4-6 CDC feathers and tie them directly to the hook shank, resulting in a much more buoyant, lifelike fly. In addition, we also incorporate a 'buggy thorax' which gives the fly the correct proportions."

CDC Caddis

Bright green version

Pattern type: Adult caddis or caddis emerger
Submitted by: English Angling Trappings (New Fairfield, Connecticut)
Originated by: Jim Krul version of Marjan Fratnick pattern
Tied by: Jim Krul

Hook: Mustad 94840, #14-#18
Thread: Tobacco Danville 6/0
Body: Cream CDC feather, tied in by tip, twisted and wrapped forward (bright green CDC for bright green version)
Wing: 2 cream CDC feathers

Comments: "This pattern," notes Jim Krul, "should be part of every tyer's program and in everyone's vest. It's proven effective fishing downstream, on a retrieve, dead drift in the surface film, and on stillwater." After wrapping the body, trim any wayward CDC fibers to produce a neat silhouette. To tie the wing, tie in a CDC feather by the butt, using loose thread wraps to affix it to the top of the shank; then pull the feather butt forward, sliding the feather beneath the thread wraps to draw the wing to the proper size. Repeat with a second feather. Sizes and colors of this pattern can be adapted to match a variety of naturals.

Chuck Caddis

Pattern type: Adult caddis
Submitted by: Backcast Fly Shop (Benzonia, Michigan)
Originated by: Eric Leiser
Tied by: Black Canyon Flies

Hook: Mustad 94840, #10-#14
Thread: Black
Body: Brown, tan, or rusty brown dubbing
Wings: Woodchuck tail
Hackle: Brown

Comments: This fly is highly successful in early and late summer, and in the fall.

Coleman's Early Adult Caddis

Front view

Pattern type: Adult caddis
Submitted by: Coleman's Fly Shop (Spencerport, New York)
Originated by: Carl Coleman
Tied by: Carl Coleman

Hook: Daiichi 1180, #14
Thread: Yellow UNI 8/0
Body: Light olive Mad River dubbing #18
Wing: Real or imitation wood duck flank, tied as tent over body
Hackle: 4-5 wraps of light ginger, clipped on bottom

Guinea Hornberg

Top view

Pattern type: Caddis adult, emerger
Submitted by: Eldredge Bros. Fly Shop (Cape Neddick, Maine)
Originated by: Wayne Bickford version of Hornberg
Tied by: Wayne Bickford

Hook: Mustad 9671, #10-#16
Thread: Black
Body: Muskrat dubbing
Wings: Natural bluish-gray feathers from guinea hen neck, tied tent-style
Hackle: Light grizzly and medium blue dun, mixed

Comments: Tyer Wayne Bickford explains, "The Guinea Hornberg can be fished dry when gray caddis are hatching, or it can be fished just under the surface for emerging caddis. The wing is tied tent-style, as in the original Hornberg. This fly has been fished successfully in many northern New England rivers."

The Hatch Combo

Top view

Pattern type: Caddis, mayfly, stonefly, grasshopper
Submitted by: The Fly Hive (North Jay, Maine)
Originated by: Steven Hatch
Tied by: Steven Hatch

Hook: Mustad 94840, #10-#18
Thread: Black 6/0 or 8/0
Body: Mukrat dubbing
Wing: Wood duck flank feather down center, brown hackle tips on each side
Hackle: Cream or white

Comments: This fly is designed to present the fish with a silhouette of various natural food forms. Says tyer Steven Hatch, "This fly works well wet or dry even though it is tied as a dry. To fish the pattern most effectively, float it as a dry and as the current starts to swing the fly around, give the line a little pull to sink the fly. Then swim it back to you. This fly has worked in 15 states, including Maine and Alaska, and has even taken striped bass off Portsmouth, New Hampshire." The pattern works best in size 12.

Jeff's Deer Hair Caddis

Versions with green body (left) and tan body (right)

Pattern type: Adult caddis
Submitted by: Steelhead Connection Custom Flies (North Muskegon, Michigan)
Originated by: Version of Elk Hair Caddis
Tied by: Jeffrey P. Bonin

Hook: Mustad 94840, #10-#20
Thread: Tan or light olive Danville 6/0
Body: Brown Antron dubbing (or color to match natural; alternate versions shown in supplementary photo)
Wing: Deer leg hair
Head: Flared and clipped butts from wing hair

Comments: Tyer Jeffrey Bonin explains, "I've adapted the Elk Hair Caddis by using deer hair, which is more readily available in our area. More importantly, I have added incredible durability to the fly by tying the head Muddler style. I comb out the soft and short fibers, stack the wing fibers, hold them firmly, then wrap through the butts of the fibers, allowing them to spin. I then whip-finish, cement the wraps, and trim the fibers.
    This pattern has outfished all other surface caddis patterns I have compared it to during my fishing/guiding on the Muskegon River over the past four years. It is simple, durable, and always produces fish."

John's 'Chuck Caddis

Pattern type:	Adult caddis
Submitted by:	Mountain Valley Flies (Solon, Maine)
Originated by:	John Kenealy
Tied by:	John Kenealy

Hook:	Mustad 94840 or other standard dry-fly, #12-#18
Thread:	Black 6/0
Body:	English hare's ear
Hackle:	Brown, palmered over body with "V" cut on top to accommodate wing
Wing:	Woodchuck guard hairs

Comments: John Kenealy notes, "I have been fishing this fly for almost 20 years all over the Northeast. It matches the zebra caddis quite well in larger sizes. It is my best all-around adult caddis pattern. It can also be tied in black, olive, and tan."

Jon's Alder Fly

Bottom view

Pattern type:	Adult caddis
Submitted by:	North Country Angler (Intervale, New Hampshire)
Originated by:	Jon Howe
Tied by:	Jon Howe

Hook:	Mustad 94833, #8-#12
Thread:	Black
Body:	Olive Antron dubbing
Ribbing:	Brown hackle, palmered; counterwrapped with green oval tinsel
Wings:	Mottled turkey tail, lacquered and cut to shape
Hackle:	Black

Comments: This pattern is tied to represent the zebra caddis, an important hatch on the Androscoggin River in New Hampshire.

Mini Mac

Pattern type:	Adult caddis or stonefly
Submitted by:	Northern Tier Outfitters (Galeton, Pennsylvania)
Originated by:	Dan MacIntosh
Tied by:	Brad Bireley

Hook:	Daiichi 1280, #8-#18
Thread:	Rusty brown 8/0
Wing:	Elk hair
Hackle:	Brown

Comments: This fly is a miniature version of the MacIntosh, an Atlantic salmon pattern. It is quick and easy to tie, floats well, and skitters easily across the water. It can be tied in a number of colors.

Moose Neck Caddis

Pattern type:	Adult caddis
Submitted by:	Thom's of Maine (Houlton, Maine)
Originated by:	Thom Willard
Tied by:	Thom Willard

Hook:	TMC 101, #12-#18
Thread:	Tan UNI 8/0
Body:	Tan turkey biot
Ribbing:	Medium dun neck hackle, tied in by butt at rear of hook, palmered; clipped on top
Wings:	Bleached moose neck hair
Hackle:	Ginger
Antennae:	Bleached moose neck hair

Mr. Magill's Caddis (Magill)

Top view

Pattern type: Adult caddis
Submitted by: The Forks Fly Shop (Inglewood, Ontario)
Originated by: Wayne F. Martin
Tied by: Wayne F. Martin

Hook: Partridge Hooper E1A L/S4, #10-#20
Thread: Gray
Underbody: Light olive rabbit dubbing, sparse
Overbody: Double layer of stripped peacock quill
Thorax: Light olive rabbit dubbing
Wing: Deer hair
Legs: Butt ends from wing, flared and clipped flat on top, trimmed to irregular lengths

Bottom view

Comments: On this fly, the wing hair is mounted atop the thorax material. Spiral the thread toward the hook eye, pulling some hair butts back with each wrap to splay the butts outward. Trim flat on top. When viewed from above, the hair butts should radiate in all directions. Clip them to uneven lengths, but keep an overall side-to-side balance so that the fly lands upright.

Preacher

Pattern type: Adult caddis
Submitted by: Dakota Angler & Outfitter (Rapid City, South Dakota)
Originated by: unknown
Tied by: Ernest Hersman

Hook: Dry fly, #12
Thread: Black Gudebrod 8/0
Body: Bronze peacock herl
Wing: Rooster pheasant rump feather treated with Flexament
Hackle: Natural dun or grizzly

Saco River Caddis

Pattern type: Adult caddis
Submitted by: North Country Angler (Intervale, New Hampshire)
Originated by: Dick Surette
Tied by: Bill Thompson

Hook: Dry fly, #12
Thread: Tan
Egg sack: Fluorescent green yarn
Body: Gray/brown fur dubbing
Ribbing: Grizzly hackle palmered over body, clipped on top
Wings: Light tan elk hair
Hackle: Brown

Comments: This pattern was designed by noted tyer Dick Surette for the Saco River in New Hampshire. "The important part of this fly," explains Bill Thompson, "is the fluorescent green egg sack. The trout will take this fly over one without the egg sack. This pattern also makes a good attractor fly with a small bead-head nymph attached as a dropper."

Spent Poly Winged Caddis

Top view

Front view

Pattern type: Spent caddis
Submitted by: Great Lakes Fly Fishing Company (Rockford, Michigan)
Originated by: unknown
Tied by: Dennis Potter

Hook: TMC 100, TMC 101, or dry-fly hook, #16-#20
Thread: Green or color to match natural
Body: Green Superfine dubbing or color to match natural
Wings: Light dun poly yarn splayed into 4 spent wings

Tan CDC/Deer Leg Caddis

Pattern type: Adult caddis
Submitted by: Wilderness Trekker
(Orwigsburg, Pennsylvania)
Originated by: Todd R. Seigfried
Tied by: Todd R. Seigfried

Hook: Dry fly, #12-#20
Thread: Dark brown 8/0
Body: Tan beaver dubbing
Legs: Spun deer hair, clipped away from top of
shank, trimmed to length below shank,
fibers bent to form leg joints
Wings: Natural gray CDC

Comments: This leg style comes from
English tyer Oliver Edwards.

Tent Wing Caddis

Comments:
This pattern was
tied for the
Muskegon River
when bushier
styles, like the Elk
Hair Caddis, failed.
It can be fished
dead drift or
dragged across
the current. Size
and color can be
altered to match a
variety of caddis
species.

Pattern type: Adult caddis
Submitted by: Flies for Michigan (N. Muskegon, Michigan)
Originated by: Al Rockwood
Tied by: Al Rockwood

Hook: TMC 101, #14-#20
Thread: Black UNI 8/0
Body: Ginger Superfine dubbing
Wings: Polyethylene sheet, patterned with
waterproof marker
Hackle: Ginger
Antennae: Black UNI 8/0 thread

TP's Little Caddis Thing

Pattern type: Adult caddis
Submitted by: Bob Mitchell's Fly Shop (Lake Elmo, Minnesota)
Originated by: Tracy Peterson
Tied by: Tracy Peterson

Hook: TMC 100, #16-#18
Thread: Gray UNI 8/0
Abdomen: One CDC feather tied in by tip at the head, twisted and
wrapped forward
Wings: 4 CDC feathers tied with tips toward rear of hook; 2
outermost feather stem butts are bent toward hook bend,
tied in position, and clipped to length
Thorax: Hare's mask or squirrel
Antennae: Pheasant tail fibers

Trump Card Caddis

Pattern type: Adult caddis or diving caddis
Submitted by: The Fish Hawk (Atlanta, Georgia)
Originated by: Robert Rooks, Jr.
Tied by: Robert Rooks, Jr.

Hook: TMC 100, #14
Thread: Tan UNI 8/0, or color to match natural
Body: Tan Nature's Spirit Dubbing, or color to
match natural
Wing: Golden Standard SLF over Hungarian
partridge fibers
Head: Tan Nature's Spirit Dubbing, or color to
match natural

Comments: Robert Rooks observes,
"The SLF overwing gives a fluttering
effect when the pattern is fished dry and
a halo effect when it is fished as a diving
adult."

Vermont Hare's Ear Caddis

Pattern type: Caddis adult or emerger
Submitted by: Classic Outfitters (South Burlington, Vermont)
Originated by: From Farrow Allen
Tied by: Rhey Plumley

Hook: Dry fly, #14-#18
Thread: Brown
Body: Hare's ear dubbing
Hackle: Grizzly and brown mixed, tied short

Comments: Tyer Rhey Plumley notes that this pattern is taken from *Vermont Trout Streams*, by Allen, Antczak, and Shea. It is a staple in northern Vermont streams and stillwaters, fished wet or dry.

CHAPTER **4**

Stoneflies

Nymphs

Bead Body Yellow Stonefly

Pattern type:	Yellow stonefly nymph
Submitted by:	Housatonic River Outfitters, Inc. (West Cornwall, Connecticut)
Originated by:	Harold McMillan
Tied by:	Harold McMillan
Hook:	Daiichi 1730, #6-#10
Thread:	Yellow Danville 6/0
Butt:	Golden yellow Wapsi Super Bright Dubbing
Tail:	Yellow goose biots
Abdomen:	Gold Killer Caddis Glass bead, size large
Abdomen:	Golden yellow Wapsi Super Bright Dubbing and (optional) two 3/16″ brass beads
Wing case:	Turkey flight feather segment
Legs:	Black goose biots
Antennae:	Yellow goose biots

Top view

Comments: This pattern can be tied with brass beads in the thorax to make a very quick-sinking fly, or they can be omitted for a slower-sinking version.

Berge's Black Stone

Pattern type:	Stonefly nymph
Submitted by:	Superior Fly Angler (Superior, Wisconsin)
Originated by:	Dick Berge
Tied by:	Dick Berge
Hook:	TMC 200R, #4; strips of .030″ lead wire lashed to sides of shank
Thread:	Black Monocord
Tail:	Black biots
Abdomen:	Gray Furryfoam
Ribbing:	Black Swannundaze or Larva Lace
Wing case:	Black Swiss Straw
Legs:	Pheasant church window feather
Thorax:	Gray Furryfoam mounted on underside of shank at rear of thorax, pulled forward on underside and tied off behind hook eye
Antennae:	Black biots

Bottom view

Blackburn Tellico Nymph

Pattern type: Stonefly nymph
Submitted by: Choo Choo Fly & Tackle (Chattanooga, Tennessee)
Originated by: Rick Blackburn
Tied by: Brad Weeks

Hook: TMC 5262, #8-#12
Thread: Olive 6/0
Tail: Wood duck flank fibers
Body: Golden Hare's Ear Plus dubbing
Ribbing: 3 peacock herls, twisted
Hackle: Brown rooster
Shellback: Turkey tail segment coated with Dave's Flexament

Brown Stone Nymph

Top view

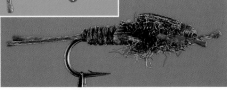

Pattern type: Stonefly nymph
Submitted by: Fly and Field (Glen Ellyn, Illinois)
Originated by: Bob Dulian
Tied by: Bob Dulian

Hook: TMC 3761, #8-#14
Thread: Rust Danville 6/0
Tail: 6lb Dacron fly line backing tinted brown with marker, lacquered
Abdomen: 10lb Dacron fly line backing tinted brown with marker
Wing case: Turkey tail, lacquered and cut to shape
Legs: 6lb Dacron fly line backing tinted brown with marker, lacquered
Thorax: Brown SLF Master Class dubbing

Delaware River Stone

Top view

Bottom view

Pattern type: Stonefly nymph
Submitted by: The Sporting Gentleman of Delaware (Centreville, Delaware)
Originated by: Unknown
Tied by: John Hendry

Hook: Mustad 79580, #4-#10; strips of lead wire lashed to sides of shank
Thread: Brown 6/0
Tail: Dacron line colored brown with waterproof marker, lacquered
Abdomen: Brown Larva Lace
Thorax: Brownish-olive dubbing
Wing cases: Mottled brown Bugskin, cut to shape
Legs: Brown New Dub, fine
Head: Butt of Bugskin from wing case
Antennae: Dacron line colored brown with waterproof marker

Comments: This heavily weighted fly was designed for fishing the bottom of riffles in the upper Delaware River system.

Double "R" Stonefly Nymph

Pattern type: Little black stonefly nymph
Submitted by: The Angler's Room (Latrobe, Pennsylvania)
Originated by: Richard Rohrbaugh
Tied by: Richard Rohrbaugh

Hook: Mustad 80250BR, #12-#14
Thread: Black
Tail: Black hackle fibers
Abdomen: Black rabbit fur dubbing with guard hairs left in
Ribbing: Fine copper wire, counterwrapped
Wing case: Black quill segment such as crow's wing
Thorax: Black rabbit fur dubbing with guard hairs ahead of gold metal bead

Comments: Tyer Richard Rohrbaugh notes that this pattern tied as a Hare's Ear nymph is also very effective.

Early Brown Stonefly Nymph

Pattern type: Stonefly nymph
Submitted by: Morning Dew Anglers (Berwick, Pennsylvania)
Originated by: Ronald J. Messimer
Tied by: Ronald J. Messimer

Hook: TMC 2312, #8
Thread: Brown 3/0
Tail: Brown goose biots
Abdomen: March Brown #2 dubbing
Shellback: Brown mallard flank, lacquered
Ribbing: Black saddle hackle, stripped; counterwrapped
Thorax: Peacock herl
Legs: Brown goose biots, knotted
Wing case: Pheasant breast feather, trimmed to shape and lacquered
Antennae: Brown goose biots

Top view

Fast Water Stone Fly

Pattern type: Stonefly nymph
Submitted by: Blue River Anglers (Schoharie, New York)
Originated by: John Murray
Tied by: John Murray

Hook: Mustad 80050BR, #8-#10; weighted
Thread: Black
Tail: Black goose biots
Abdomen: Black Vinyl Rib
Wing case: Black Swiss straw
Thorax: Black chenille
Legs: 3 turns of black saddle hackle, clipped

Comments: This pattern is fished deep, dead drift. It is effective in Northeast rivers and streams with populations of stonefly nymphs and is also tied in yellow and brown.

Giant Black Stone

Top view

Pattern type: Stonefly nymph
Submitted by: Superior Fly Angler (Superior, Wisconsin)
Originated by: Matthew Paulson
Tied by: Matthew Paulson

Hook: Mustad 9672, #2-#6; weighted with.030″ lead wire
Thread: Black 6/0
Tail: 20lb Dacron fly-line backing colored black
Body: Black Hare-Tron or similar dubbing
Ribbing: Black Swannundaze
Wing case: Black Swiss straw
Legs: Knotted pheasant tail fibers
Eyes: Black mono eyes
Head: Swiss straw from wing case
Antennae: 20lb Dacron fly-line backing colored black

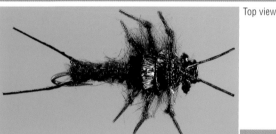

Bottom view

Comments: The tails, wing cases, and antennae are coated with Dave's Flexament.

Golden Stonefly Nymph

Comments: To weight the hook, wrap lead wire around the shank and flatten with pliers. Wrap the lead lightly with 3/0 thread, coat with lacquer, and allow to dry before dressing the fly.

Pattern type: Golden stonefly nymph
Submitted by: Morning Dew Anglers (Berwick, Pennsylvania)
Originated by: Ronald J. Messimer
Tied by: Ronald J. Messimer

Hook: TMC 2312, #8; weighted
Thread: Yellow 3/0
Tail: Yellow turkey biots
Abdomen: Pale yellow dubbing
Shellback: Yellow turkey biots, lacquered
Ribbing: White saddle hackle, stripped; counterwrapped
Thorax: Yellow ostrich herl
Legs: Yellow turkey biots, knotted
Wing case: Wood duck flank feather, trimmed to shape and lacquered
Antennae: Yellow turkey biots

Top view

Hester's Black Stone Nymph

Pattern type: Stonefly nymph
Submitted by: Chesapeake Fly & Bait Company (Arnold, Maryland)
Originated by: Jim Hester
Tied by: Jim Hester

Hook: Mustad 9672, #6-#10
Thread: Black Danville Flymaster 6/0
Tail: Black round rubber
Abdomen: Mixture of black rabbit and brown opossum dubbing, guard hairs left in; picked out between ribbing wraps
Ribbing: Transparent black Swannundaze, counterwrapped
Thorax: A few wraps of pearlescent black Cactus Chenille
Legs: Black fine round rubber

Comments: This pattern should be heavily weighted; it can also be tied in olive, brown, and amber.

Joe's Stone

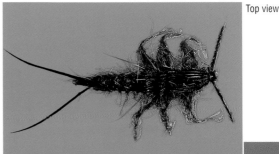

Top view

Bottom view

Pattern type: Stonefly nymph
Submitted by: Delaware River Outfitters (Pennington, New Jersey)
Originated by: Joe Sacchetti
Tied by: Joe Sacchetti

Hook: Long-shank nymph hook, #8-#14
Thread: 6/0 color to match natural
Tail: Black goose biots
Abdomen: Dyed squirrel fur or rabbit mask
Ribbing: Stripped peacock herl
Wing case: Turkey tail segment
Thorax: Abdomen dubbing spun in dubbing loop
Legs: Thorax dubbing, cemented to shape

Comments: Note that the thorax on this fly is dressed in 3 sections, that is, dubbing is applied and the wing case material folded three times. To form the legs, Joe Sacchetti explains, "Pick out the hair of the thorax section so it extends evenly to each side. Take a toothpick and apply head cement to the last half of the leg hairs. Use the toothpick to separate individual legs. I also fold the legs over a length of heavy monofilament. The mono keeps all the leg joints on one side of the body even. When the cement is firm, remove the mono."

Krom's Stonefly

Front view

Pattern type: Stonefly nymph
Submitted by: Doc's Custom Tackle (Portage, Michigan)
Originated by: Charles Krom
Tied by: Merrill S. Katz

Hook: Mustad 9672, #10-#14
Thread: Black (Danville #100) 6/0 prewaxed
Tail: 2 peccary fibers
Underbody: White floss
Abdomen: 2 stripped peacock quills
Ribbing: Fine gold wire counterwrapped over abdomen
Thorax: Peacock herl
Wing case: Segment of gray mallard quill
Legs: Poor-quality brown dry-fly hackle, folded and palmered over thorax, trimmed on bottom

Comments: "This fly," notes tyer Merrill Katz, "was developed for fishing the streams of Westchester County and New York's Catskill rivers. It has been effective in Pennsylvania streams and is especially useful on the high-gradient streams of the Smokey Mountains. It is best fished quartering downstream in gentle riffles. A micro-shot fastened above the fly allows the pattern to be fished with greater effectiveness in pools. It has also been a good general stonefly imitation on Midwestern waters." After attaching the tails and ribbing, Katz uses white floss to form a cigar-shaped underbody over the length of the shank. The two quills for the abdomen are wrapped simultaneously and given two coats of lacquer after the fly is complete.

Matt's Golden Stone

Top view

Bottom view

Pattern type: Stonefly nymph
Submitted by: The Superior Fly Angler (Superior, Wisconsin)
Originated by: Matt Paulson
Tied by: Matt Paulson

Hook: Mustad 9672, #6-#10; weighted heavily with .025" lead wire
Thread: Tan 6/0
Tail: 20lb white dacron line, colored with water proof markers, coated with Flexament
Body: Hare-Tron golden stone blend dubbing
Ribbing: Clear Swannundaze or Larva Lace, colored on back side with brown marker
Wing case: Swiss straw, mottled with waterproof marker and lacquered
Legs: Knotted pheasant tail fibers, coated with Flexament
Antennae: 20lb white Dacron line, colored with waterproof markers, coated with Flexament

Comments: Mono eyes can be added to this pattern if desired. It should be fished very deep.

Mike's Stone

Top view

Front view

Pattern type: Stonefly nymph
Submitted by: River's Edge Fly Shop (Thunder Bay, Ontario)
Originated by: Scott E. Smith and Mike Sewards
Tied by: Scott E. Smith

Hook: TMC 5263, #10-#12
Thread: Black UNI 6/0
Tail: Black goose biots
Abdomen: Brown dubbing
Ribbing: Black balloon strip
Wing case: Turkey quill segment, lacquered
Legs: Grouse feather
Thorax: Black ostrich herl
Antennae (opt.): Black goose biots

Comments: To form the legs on this pattern, tie in the wing case material. Atop the wing case mounting wraps, tie in a grouse feather by the tip. Dress the thorax. Pull the grouse feather forward and tie off behind the hook eye. Bring wing case over top of grouse feather and tie off.

Mike's Stonefly

Pattern type: Stonefly nymph
Submitted by: Great Lakes Outfitters (Tonawanda, New York)
Originated by: Michael Donohue
Tied by: Michael Donohue

Hook: Wet-fly or nymph hook, #8-#12
Thread: Olive
Tail: Brown goose biots
Body: Light tan Antron dubbing
Hackle: Grizzly

Comments: "Though tied as a stonefly pattern," Michael Donohue points out, "this fly represents other aquatic life as well. It is one of our most popular flies and has accounted for many fish. Though best fished as a nymph, it also fishes well wet-fly style."

Mr. Stony

Top view

Pattern type: Stonefly nymph
Submitted by: Adventure Fly Fishing (Greensboro, North Carolina)
Originated by: Jeff Wilkins
Tied by: Jeff Wilkins

Hook: TMC 200R, #6-#10
Thread: Yellow 6/0
Underbody: 2 strips lead wire lashed to sides of shank
Tail: Black goose biots
Body: Golden stone Umpqua Sparkleblend dubbing
Shellback: Turkey tail segment
Ribbing: 0x tippet material or 15lb mono
Legs: Mottled hen back
Wing case: Turkey tail segments
Head: Turkey tail segment from second wing case, doubled back and tied down

Comments: This is a favorite early season searching pattern for small streams; it should be fished on the bottom.

Peacock Stone

Pattern type: Black stonefly nymph
Submitted by: Backcast Fly Shop (Benzonia, Michigan)
Originated by: Jeff Bonin
Tied by: Jeff Bonin

Hook: Mustad 37160, #6-#10
Thread: Black
Tail: Black goose biots
Body: Peacock herl
Legs: Black hackle
Wing case: Turkey quill

Comments: This fly is productive in the Betsie and Platte rivers in northwest Michigan.

Peccary Body Stonefly/Mayfly Nymph

Pattern type: Stonefly or mayfly nymph
Submitted by: English Angling Trappings (New Fairfield, Connecticut)
Originated by: Jim Krul
Tied by: Justin Krul

Hook: Mustad 9671, #10-#18
Thread: Black UNI 6/0
Tail: Peccary fiber tips
Abdomen: Peccary fiber
Wing case: Black Swiss straw
Thorax: Black UNI Mohair

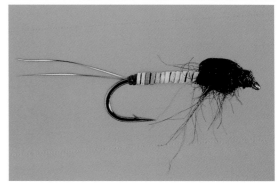

Comments: This pattern is easy to tie and can be modified to match various naturals.

Prairie River Stonefly

Pattern type: Stonefly nymph
Submitted by: The Fly Fishers (West Allis, Wisconsin)
Originated by: Pat Ehlers
Tied by: Pat Ehlers

Hook: TMC 205BL, #8-#10
Thread: Black 8/0
Tail: Black goose biots
Abdomen: Black dubbing
Ribbing: Black Larva Lace, counterwrapped
Wing case: Black Swiss straw
Thorax: Black rabbit fur strip spun in dubbing loop, trimmed top and bottom

Front view

Ryan's Double Bead Stonefly (Brown)

Pattern type: Stonefly nymph
Submitted by: Choo Choo Fly & Tackle (Chattanooga, Tennessee)
Originated by: Ryan Meulemans
Tied by: Ryan Meulemans

Hook: TMC 2302, #6-#10
Thread: Brown 6/0
Tail: Brown goose biots
Abdomen: Brown Antron dubbing, picked out
Ribbing: Brown Larva Lace
Thorax: 2 copper beads
Wing case: Turkey quill
Hackle: Brown grizzly, clipped on top

Small Stonefly Nymph

Pattern type: Stonefly nymph
Submitted by: South Mountain Custom Rod & Tackle
(Lebanon, Pennsylvania)
Originated by: Jim Yurejefcic
Tied by: Jim Yurejefcic

Hook: Mustad 3906B, Mustad 9671,
or Mustad 9672, #10-#16
Thread: Black 6/0
Tail: Black goose biots
Body: Black ostrich herl
Wing case: Peacock herl
Hackle: Soft black hen saddle fibers

Comments: "This pattern," says Jim Yurejefcic, "had its start on the
Salmon River in upstate New York, where we used it for steelhead.
Since that time, I and many others have fished it all over
Pennsylvania, West Virginia, New York, and on streams in the West.
The pattern works well wherever there are stoneflies. You can alter
the size of the pattern by changing hooks; this is the reason for the
number of different hooks in the recipe. The pattern can also be tied
in brown and gold depending on what color of stonefly you wish to
imitate."

Simple All Purpose Black Nymph

Pattern type: Stonefly or mayfly nymph
Submitted by: English Angling Trappings (New Fairfield, Connecticut)
Originated by: Jim Krul
Tied by: Justin Krul

Hook: Mustad 9671, #10-#18
Thread: Black UNI 6/0
Tail: Black UNI Mohair
Abdomen: Black UNI Mohair
Wing case: Black Swiss straw
Thorax: Black UNI Mohair
Legs: Black Mohair, picked out from thorax

Comments: "This pattern," notes Jim Krul, "was designed for sim-
plicity, not only to tie, but to teach kids and beginners proportions
and body patterns for nymphs. It has proven effective in all
Northeast streams." It can also be tied in brown and tan.

Spring Stone

Pattern type: Stonefly nymph
Submitted by: River's Edge Fly Shop (Thunder Bay, Ontario)
Originated by: Scott E. Smith
Tied by: Scott E. Smith

Hook: TMC 5263, #4-#10
Thread: Black UNI 6/0
Tail: Red fox squirrel tail
Body: Black chenille
Ribbing: Gold oval tinsel
Wing case: Red fox squirrel tail
Legs: Brown neck hackle palmered over thorax
Antennae: Red fox squirrel tail from wing case

Thinskin Stone

Top view

Bottom view

Top view of black version with Flexi-Floss tails and antennae

Pattern type: Stonefly nymph
Submitted by: Riverbend Sport Shop (Southfield, Michigan)
Originated by: Matt Reid version of Randall Kaufmann pattern
Tied by: Matt Reid

Hook: TMC 200R, #4-#10
Thread: Dark brown 6/0
Tail: Cranberry goose biots (or brown Flexi-Floss)
Body: Brown Kaufmann Stonefly Blend (or black, or Angora substitute)
Shellback: Mottled oak Wapsi Thinskin
Ribbing: 4x tippet material or clear mono
Wing cases: Mottled oak Wapsi Thinskin
Legs: Mottled hen hackle tied in by tip over wing case mount, pulled forward over thorax, tied off
Antennae: Cranberry goose biots (or brown Flexi-Floss)

Tunghead Winter Stonefly Nymph

Top view

Pattern type: Black winter stonefly nymph
Submitted by: Bob Mitchell's Fly Shop (Lake Elmo, Minnesota)
Originated by: Murry Humble
Tied by: Murry Humble

Hook: TMC 200R, #10
Thread: Black 6/0
Tail: Black goose biots
Body: Black Krystal Dub
Ribbing: Black medium Vinyl Rib, counterwrapped
Wing case: Black turkey quill
Legs: Black Rainy's small round rubber
Head: 5/32" black tungsten bead underwrapped with lead wire
Antennae: 2 strands black Krystal Flash

Comments: This fly is tied "upside-down" since it will turn over and ride point-up in the water.

Wake-Up Call

Pattern type: Stonefly nymph, *Isonychia* nymph, general attractor
Submitted by: The Sporting Gentleman (Media, Pennsylvania)
Originated by: Tom Fink
Tied by: Tom Fink

Hook: TMC 200R, #16
Thread: Orange UNI 8/0
Tail: Black marabou topped with peacock herl tips
Body: Peacock herl from tail, twisted around thread and wrapped
Ribbing: Webby black rooster neck hackle, palmered over body
Head: 3/32" black tungsten bead

Comments: Tyer Tom Fink notes that this fly successfully imitates many food forms besides stonefly and *Isonychia* nymphs: dobsonfly and damselfly larvae, small leeches, small minnows, cased caddis, green and brown drake nymphs, sunken caterpillars, and sculpin. Because of the hook design, the tail will not foul around the shank.

Yellow Stone Nymph

Pattern type: Stonefly nymph
Submitted by: Flies for Michigan (N. Muskegon, Michigan)
Originated by: Al Rockwood
Tied by: Al Rockwood

Hook: Mustad 9672, #10; weighted with .025" non-toxic wire
Thread: Brown UNI 8/0
Tail: Yellow goose biots
Body: Rust leech yarn
Wing case: Turkey flight feather
Legs: Furnace hackle palmered over thorax, trimmed flush with body on top

Comments: This pattern—"my favorite for summer trout," says Al Rockwood, is easy to tie. It should be fished deep on a dead drift. It can also be tied in black.

Adults

Early Black Stone

Pattern type:	Early black stonefly adult
Submitted by:	The Sporting Gentleman (Media, Pennsylvania)
Originated by:	Jim McAndrew
Tied by:	Jim McAndrew
Hook:	Dry fly, #14
Thread:	Olive 8/0
Tail:	Oversize dun hackle, folded; tied in by tip slightly down hook bend and wrapped to point just above hook barb; clipped to "V" on bottom
Body:	4 peacock herls
Wing:	Mule deer body hair
Hackle:	Brown
Head:	Clipped wing butts

Top view

Comments: On eastern Pennsylvania streams, about the first week in February through April, from early to late afternoon, large numbers of fish rise to early black stoneflies. Jim McAndrew designed this pattern for the stonefly hatch. It is also effective in imitating other high-floating naturals, such as caddis and craneflies.

Early Black Stonefly

Pattern type:	Adult stonefly
Submitted by:	Northern Tier Outfitters (Galeton, Pennsylvania)
Originated by:	Brad Bireley
Tied by:	Brad Bireley
Hook:	Daiichi 1180, #16-#18
Thread:	Black 8/0
Body:	Fine black dubbing
Wings:	Dark dun turkey biots
Hackle:	Grizzly

Top view

Early Brown Stone

Pattern type:	Brown stonefly adult
Submitted by:	The Sporting Gentleman (Media, Pennsylvania)
Originated by:	unknown
Tied by:	Jim McAndrew
Hook:	Dry fly, #14
Thread:	Olive 8/0
Body:	Pheasant tail fibers
Ribbing:	Brown hackle, palmered over body, clipped flat on top
Wing:	Dun hackle with long barbs (see "Comments")

Comments: To dress the wing, pull the hackle barbs to the butt of the feather to make an oval wing with a veined appearance. Tie in and clip the tip to length.

Egg-Laying Early Black Stone

Pattern type:	Early black stonefly adult
Submitted by:	Fly Angler (Fridley, Minnesota)
Originated by:	Chris Hansen
Tied by:	Chris Hansen
Hook:	2XL dry fly, #10-#14
Thread:	Dark brown 6/0
Egg sac:	Pearl/blue Lite Brite
Body:	Black deer hair, spun and clipped
Wings:	Grizzly hackle tips
Hackle:	Grizzly and brown, mixed

Front view

Comments:
Chris Hansen notes, "In late March on Wisconsin's Kinnickinnic River, I encountered a large number of stoneflies on the

Top view

water. This was the first year that the season was open in March, so I wasn't prepared with the proper pattern. After several attempts with different designs, I settled on this as being the best. It floats great, but rides low. Brown trout really go for it when black stoneflies are laying eggs. Sometimes skating or skittering works better than a dead drift."

Evergreen Lime Sally

Front view

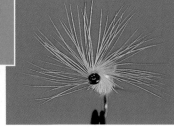

Pattern type: Adult little green stonefly (Chloroperlidae family)
Submitted by: Evergreen Fly Fishing Company (Clarksburg, West Virginia)
Originated by: Franklin Oliverio
Tied by: Ken Long

Hook: Dry fly, #18-#20
Thread: White or cream 6/0 or 8/0
Tail: 2 moose body hairs
Body: Chartreuse or lime fur or synthetic dubbing
Wing: White Swiss straw, cut to shape
Hackle: Ginger, clipped on bottom

Comments: According to Franklin Oliverio, the lime sally is "a super hatch" on many West Virginia streams. In this pattern, the tails are separated by a ball of dubbing. The wing is formed by cutting the Swiss straw into a 1/8" strip; the wing should extend just beyond the hook bend.

Bottom view

John's Golden Stonefly

Comments: Tyer John Kenealy explains, "I originated John's Golden Stonefly about 18 years ago to imitate stonefly hatches on New York's Beaverkill River. I have since fished it successfully all over the Northeast. It has produced very well on Maine's Kennebec River and the East and West Branches of the Penobscot. It is fished in the normal manner for adult stoneflies."

Pattern type: Stonefly adult
Submitted by: Mountain Valley Flies (Solon, Maine)
Originated by: John Kenealy
Tied by: John Kenealy

Hook: Mustad 94840 or other standard dry-fly, #6-#10
Thread: Black 6/0
Body: Yellow rabbit
Ribbing: Brown hackle palmered over body
Wing: Gray squirrel tail
Hackle: Brown and grizzly, mixed

Little "T" Stonefly

Pattern type: Adult early brown and early black stonefly
Submitted by: Evergreen Fly Fishing Company (Clarksburg, West Virginia)
Originated by: Franklin Oliverio
Tied by: Ken Long

Hook: Dry fly, #12-#16
Thread: Dark brown 8/0
Tail: 2 moose body hairs, widely split
Body: 3 or 4 pheasant tail fibers
Wing: 3 clumps stiff dark dun hackle barbs
Hackle: Dark dun

Comments: This fly can be fished dead drift or skittered across the surface. It should be hackled heavily. On many Eastern waters, these small dark stoneflies provide some of the earliest dry-fly fishing of the year.

Twisted Butt Yellow Sally

Pattern type: Adult yellow sally stonefly
Submitted by: Dakota Angler & Outfitter (Rapid City, South Dakota)
Originated by: Hans Stephenson
Tied by: Hans Stephenson

Hook: Partridge CS27, #16-#18
Thread: Tan 10/0
Abdomen: Yellow rug yarn, furled; red egg sac colored with marker
Thorax: SLF Masterclass dubbing, #12
Wing: Bleached elk hair
Antennae: Elk hair from wing

Comments: To form a furled body, see "Comments" under "Antron Damsel Nymph," p. 95.

CHAPTER 5

Midges, Cranefly, Blackfly, and Alderfly

Midges

Bead Head Chironomid

Pattern type: Chironomid pupa
Submitted by: The Fly Fishers (West Allis, Wisconsin)
Originated by: Pat Ehlers
Tied by: Pat Ehlers

Hook: TMC 3761, #10-#18
Thread: Black 8/0
Tail: White Polar Aire
Abdomen: Black Micro Larva Lace
Wing case: Black Swiss straw
Abdomen: Peacock herl
Head: 3/32" black bead
Antennae: White Polar Aire

Comments: The antennae are mounted first on this pattern, and the bead then slipped over the hook shank. The fly is completed by binding the wingcase behind the bead head and whip-finishing between the thorax and wingcase.

Bob's Midge

Pattern type: Adult midge
Submitted by: Oak Orchard Fly Shop (Williamsville, New York)
Originated by: Bob Morrissey
Tied by: Bob Morrissey

Hook: TMC 101, #26
Thread: Black 14/0
Body: Black tying thread
Wings: Zing wing material
Legs: Black Chinese boar fibers

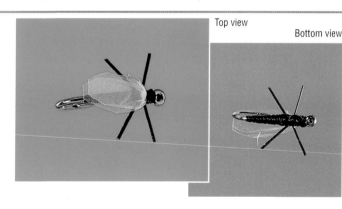

Top view

Bottom view

Coleman's Shucking Pupa (Spring Creek)

Pattern type: Midge pupa
Submitted by: Coleman's Fly Shop (Spencerport, New York)
Originated by: Carl Coleman
Tied by: Rick Tabor

Hook: Daiichi 1110, #20
Thread: Black UNI 8/0
Shuck: Z-Wing strip, 1/8" wide
Abdomen: 2 layers black tying thread
Ribbing: White 3/0 Monocord, counterwrapped
Wings: 2 short pieces of Spirit River Celo-Z-Wing
Thorax: Muskrat dubbing

Comments: The abdomen and ribbing on this pattern are coated with vinyl cement. This pattern is effective when cast to rising trout, letting it swing, and giving it a twitch.

Daphnia Cluster Midge

Pattern type: Daphnia, cluster midge
Submitted by: Steelhead Connection Custom Flies (North Muskegon, Michigan)
Originated by: Adapted from Gary Borger's version of Griffith's Gnat
Tied by: Jeffrey P. Bonin

Hook: Mustad 94838, #18-#22
Thread: Cream or white Danville Flymaster 6/0
Body: Clear Antron, loosely dubbed
Hackle: Grizzly, 2 or 3 turns through body, clipped

Comments: This cluster midge pattern works well when *Daphnia* are present. It was designed for Michigan's Muskegon River.

Deer Hair Emerging Palomino

Pattern type: Midge pupa
Submitted by: Dakota Angler & Outfitter (Rapid City, South Dakota)
Originated by: Dave Einerwold version of Brett Smith design
Tied by: Dave Gamet

Hook: Daiichi 1150, #16-#24
Thread: Black
Abdomen: Black New Dub
Wing: Short, coarse whitetail deer hair
Thorax: Black Fine and Dry dubbing

Foam Head Midge

Pattern type: Adult midge
Submitted by: Choo Choo Fly & Tackle (Chattanooga, Tennessee)
Originated by: Ryan Meulemans
Tied by: Ryan Meulemans

Hook: TMC 2487, #16-#18
Thread: Black 8/0
Tail: 2 strands pearl Krystal Flash
Body: Wapsi Sow/Scud dubbing, "Sowbug" color
Wings: White closed-cell foam

Comments: Originator Ryan Meulemans says, "I designed this fly for the midge hatches on the Clinch River near Knoxville, Tennessee. The benefit of this fly is that you are representing #20-#24 midges on a #16 hook. The white foam makes the fly highly visible, and dubbing color can be adjusted to match other naturals."

Hester's Little White Larva

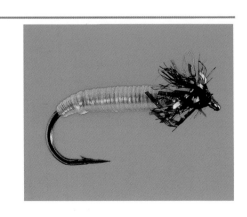

Pattern type: Midge larva
Submitted by: Chesapeake Fly & Bait Company (Arnold, Maryland)
Originated by: Jim Hester
Tied by: Jim Hester

Hook: Wet fly, #12-#14; weight, optional
Thread: Black Danville Flymaster 6/0
Body: White Lumi-Flex or UNI-Stretch
Legs: 1 to 1 1/2 wraps pearlescent black Micro Cactus Chenille

John's Spring Creek Pupa

Pattern type: Midge pupa
Submitted by: Coleman's Fly Shop (Spencerport, New York)
Originated by: John Abiuso
Tied by: John Abiuso

Hook: Daiichi 1150 scud/caddis, #16; or Daiichi 1140, #18–#20
Thread: Black UNI 8/0
Abdomen: Black tying thread
Ribbing: Fine silver wire
Wing: Hi-Vis or Lite Brite
Thorax: Black Antron dubbing
Head: Silver metal bead

Olive Biot Midge Nymph

Pattern type: Midge pupa
Submitted by: Delaware River Outfitters (Pennington, New Jersey)
Originated by: Chris Sacchetti
Tied by: Chris Sacchetti

Hook: Daiichi Pupa, #20
Thread: Gray 8/0
Abdomen: Light olive turkey biot
Wing case: Mallard flank
Thorax: Muskrat dubbing

Comments: Tyer Chris Sacchetti notes that wrapping the biot over a thread base coated with Super Glue improves durability. Note that the biot is mounted so that the fringe-like barbules form a rib on the abdomen. This is an excellent dropper fly and works well on most spring creeks.

Utility Midge

Pattern type: Midge pupa
Submitted by: The Fish Hawk (Atlanta, Georgia)
Originated by: Robert Rooks, Jr.
Tied by: Robert Rooks, Jr.

Hook: TMC 100 or TMC 101, #18–#24
Thread: Black UNI 8/0
Shuck: White 3/0 UNI-Thread, frayed
Body: Black 8/0 UNI-Thread, built up
Ribbing: White 3/0 UNI-Thread, twisted and counterwrapped
Wings: Light gray poly yarn
Legs: White UNI 3/0

Comments: This pattern can be fished deep, or you can treat the wing and back with floatant and fish it in the surface film.

Cranefly

Orange Cranefly

Pattern type: Cranefly emerger
Submitted by: Nestor's Sporting Goods, Inc. (Quakertown and Whitehall, Pennsylvania)
Originated by: Dan Buss
Tied by: Dan Buss

Hook: TMC 100, #16–#20
Thread: Light Cahill UNI 8/0
Tail: Light dun Micro Fibetts
Body: Orange Danville 3/0 Monocord, coated with head cement
Hackle: Medium dun dry-fly hackle, tied in by tip, folded and wrapped wet-fly style

Comments: Tyer Dan Buss explains, "I developed this fly for the local limestone streams, which have prolific cranefly hatches from late April into July. The craneflies are difficult to imitate because they are so thin; that's why only thread is used to construct the body. Other body colors that work well are pale yellow and gray."

Blackfly

Blackfly Larva

Pattern type: Blackfly (*simulium*) larva
Submitted by: Adventure Fly Fishing (Greensboro, North Carolina)
Originated by: Jeff Wilkins
Tied by: Jeff Wilkins

Hook: TMC 2487, #16-#20
Thread: White UNI 8/0
Tag: 8-10 wraps fine silver wire
Body: Olive damsel Umpqua Sparkleblend dubbing
(or substitute Antron dubbing)
Anal brushes: White CDC feather tip

Comments: "This pattern," observes Jeff Wilkins, "was developed for fishing the tailwaters of the Southeast, most notably Virginia and Tennessee. These insects are widespread, but very little information or patterns covering them are available. They are a major influence during the winter and spring months. White thread is used for the body so as not to alter the color once the fly is damp. Other effective colors are gray, tan, and black. This fly is a must for a number of streams."

Alderfly

K.T.'s Alder Fly

Pattern type: Adult alderfly
Submitted by: Aardvark Outfitters (Farmington, Maine)
Originated by: Kris Thompson
Tied by: Kris Thompson

Hook: Standard dry-fly hook, #10
Thread: Dark brown 8/0
Abdomen: Pheasant tail fibers
Thorax: Peacock herl
Ribbing: 2 brown hackle feathers, palmered, clipped on top
Wings: Mottled brown turkey quill, lacquered
Antennae: 2 or 3lb Maxima Chameleon tippet material, clipped to 1 1/2"

Top view

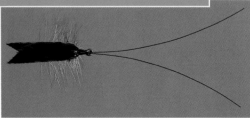

Comments: This pattern was designed for the Rangeley Region of Maine, for fishing in early to mid-July. "It is most effective," says Kris Thompson, "when adult alderflies are seen on the water. It is deadly fished near the edge of the bank where fish will congregate, especially during breezy days when adult flies are blown on the water in clusters from the shelter of the alders. The palmered hackle allows the fly to float very well, but have a low profile in the water. Because it floats low, the antennae are also on the water." The hackle on this pattern can also be trimmed even with the hook point.

CHAPTER 6

Damselfly, Dragonfly, Hellgrammites, and Crustaceans

Damselfly and Dragonfly

Antron Damsel Nymph

Pattern type: Damselfly nymph
Submitted by: Fly and Field (Glen Ellyn, Illinois)
Originated by: Steve Sato
Tied by: Steve Sato

Hook: TMC 200R, #12; at a point 3 "hook-eye" lengths behind the eye, bend hook upward 15 degrees
Thread: Olive 6/0
Tail: End of furled body, tied off with thread, clipped and frayed
Body: Olive Antron yarn, furled
Legs: 10-12 strands olive deer hair
Wing case: Olive Swiss straw
Eyes: Olive glass beads on 50lb mono

Comments:
Steven Sato notes that he borrowed the furled body style from tyer Darrel Martin. To make the body, hold a length of yarn between the thumb and forefinger of both hands. Twist the ends of the yarn in opposite directions. Move the two ends together and the yarn will twist around itself, or "furl." Pinch the base of the furl and mount the twisted yarn on the shank. Sato notes that this leg style comes from English tyer Oliver Edwards. To form the legs, crumple the deer hair and clip any "loops" that it forms. Spin the hair in a dubbing loop, wrap around shank, and bend legs to shape.

Top view

Ostrich Herl Dragonfly Nymph

Pattern type: Dragonfly nymph
Submitted by: Fly and Field (Glen Ellyn, Illinois)
Originated by: Steve Sato
Tied by: Steve Sato

Hook: TMC 7999 or Mustad 36890, #10
Thread: Black 6/0
Body: 7 strands olive ostrich herl, 3 strands peacock herl, and a length of black 3/0 tying thread, twisted and wrapped
Legs: Speckled hen or partridge, dyed olive
Wing case: Olive Swiss straw
Eyes: 1/8" black metal beads on 50lb monofilament (or substitute tungsten or glass beads)

Top view

Hellgrammites

Brad's Hellgrammite

Pattern type: Hellgrammite
Submitted by: Northern Tier Outfitters (Galeton, Pennsylvania)
Originated by: Brad Bireley
Tied by: Brad Bireley

Hook: Daiichi 2220, #2-#8; weighted with lead wire
Thread: Black 6/0
Tail: Black wool, divided
Abdomen: Black wool
Abdominal gills: Black ostrich herl, wrapped
Shellback: Black Bugskin
Ribbing: Copper wire
Wingcase: Black Bugskin from shellback
Thorax: Dave Whitlock Plus SLF #15 Dark Stone dubbing
Legs: Black emu, wrapped
Pincers: Black goose biots

Hellgrammite

Comments: This fly was modeled after a pattern that tyer Todd Seigfried found, and promptly lost, 15 years ago. Ten years later, he reconstructed this version from memory.

Pattern type:	Hellgrammite
Submitted by:	Wilderness Trekker (Orwigsburg, Pennsylvania)
Originated by:	Todd R. Seigfried
Tied by:	Todd R. Seigfried

Hook:	Streamer 4XL, #6-#12; weighted with .025" lead wire on front 1/3 of shank
Thread:	Black 6/0
Tail:	Tips of 2 gray pheasant aftershaft feathers
Body:	Gray pheasant aftershaft feathers
Ribbing:	Black hackle, clipped short
Wing case:	Black raffia or Swiss Straw
Legs:	Black hackle palmered over thorax and slightly clipped
Antennae:	Small black round rubber leg material

Rofi's Go-Devil

Top view

Comments: "This fly," notes Rob Fightmaster, "was originally designed to catch smallmouth bass on Elkhorn Creek. While it has done that well, it has also proven an effective trout pattern on the Cumberland River. Fished most often on a dead drift, it is also effective fished on the swing in faster water. Ostrich herl and rubber leg material give this fly a nice 'waggle' in the water. 'Go-Devil' is a long-time central and eastern Kentucky term for 'hellgrammite.'"

Pattern type:	Hellgrammite
Submitted by:	The Sporting Tradition (Lexington, Kentucky)
Originated by:	Rob Fightmaster
Tied by:	Rob Fightmaster

Hook:	TMC 200R, #2-#8
Thread:	Black 6/0
Tail:	Medium dun ostrich herl
Abdomen:	Dubbing blend of gray rabbit, black rabbit, gray squirrel tail, black Antron yarn, gray Antron yarn, black Lite Brite, silver Lite Brite
Shellback:	Dark gray Swiss straw
Ribbing:	Medium copper wire
Wing case:	Dark gray Swiss straw from shellback
Legs:	Brown goose biots
Thorax:	Abdomen dubbing alternating with 2 gold metal beads (size appropriate to hook)
Antennae/ pinchers:	Medium black rubber legs

Crustaceans

Andy's Sparkle Shrimp

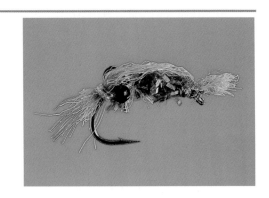

Pattern type:	Freshwater shrimp
Submitted by:	The Fly Fishing Shop (Far Hills, New Jersey)
Originated by:	Andy Sutton
Tied by:	Andy Sutton

Hook:	Orvis 1639-00, #14
Thread:	Ultra Fine Translucent thread
Body:	Olive or tan Crystal Chenille, small
Shellback:	Olive or tan Neer Hair
Eyes:	Black mono barbell eyes
Antennae:	Olive or tan Super Hair

Baby Crab

Top view

Pattern type: Newborn crayfish
Submitted by: Orleans Outdoor (Albion, New York)
Originated by: Mark Stothard
Tied by: Mark Stothard

Hook: Daiichi 1150, #8-#12; keel weighted with .030" lead wire
Thread: White, light tan, or light olive 8/0 or 12/0
Tail: Scud Back from shellback
Body: Translucent Dubbing, 85% white, 5% olive, 5% brown, 5% pink, blended
Shellback: Clear Scud Back or Body Stretch (or olive, dun or brown)
Ribbing: Olive or brown 2lb to 6lb monofilament
Eyes: Melted monofilament
Legs, feelers, and pincers: Wisps of body dubbing, picked out

Comments: "The Baby Crab," says shop owner Ron Bierstine, "is tied to imitate a newly hatched soft-shell crayfish. Nearly all streams contain crayfish that continually hatch, and opportunistic trout find the pattern hard to resist. To imitate the backward motion of the natural, the fly is tied so that the head is at the rear of the hook. Tied in larger sizes, this fly is very effective for large predatory trout. Larger patterns should be tied in darker hues."

Epoxy Back Sowbug

Top view

Pattern type: Sowbug
Submitted by: Dakota Angler & Outfitter (Rapid City, South Dakota)
Originated by: Dave Gamet
Tied by: Dave Gamet

Hook: Daiichi 1530, #12-#18
Thread: Black
Body: 1 strand gray ostrich herl and 1 light dun hen hackle, wrapped around shank
Dorsal vein: Thin Mylar tinsel or black Krystal Flash or both
Shellback: Mottled olive-bustard Thin Skin, cut to elliptical shape with tab at each end; coated with 5-minute epoxy

Comments: On this pattern, the shellback and vein material are tied in at the rear of the hook. After dressing the body, pull the Thin Skin over the back and tie off. Pull the vein material along the center of the back, tie off, and coat with epoxy.

Holt's Spring Brook Scud (Orange)

Pattern type: Scud
Submitted by: Coleman's Fly Shop (Spencerport, New York)
Originated by: Lynn Holt
Tied by: Rick Tabor

Comments: Tyer Rick Tabor notes, "This fly was developed by Rochester, NY angler Lynn Holt about 1970. Originally tied in pink, this fly has been a consistent trout-catcher world wide since its invention." To dress the pattern, lay a base of thread on the shank. Lay the straight edge of the lead half-moon atop the shank and affix it with thread, making a humped underbody, and cover

Hook: Daiichi 1550, #10-#18
Thread: Fluorescent orange Danville 6/0
Underbody: Strip of Twist-on flat lead, trimmed to half-moon shape tied on edge to top of shank
Body: Orange rabbit fur
Ribbing: Fine gold or silver wire, or extra fine gold or silver oval tinsel
Shellback: Clear 1/8" Scud Back or 1/8" plastic sheet
Legs: Orange ostrich herl

with tying thread. Palmer the dubbing over the underbody, leaving gaps; the ostrich herl is palmered forward to cover these gaps. The pattern can also be tied in pink, red, olive, and gray.

Jeff's Spiny Midge

Comments: "Spiny water fleas," observes Jeffrey Bonin, "are actually a tiny crustacean and another of our invading exotic species, introduced through ocean ballast water. They appear to be here to stay. I noticed them in the trout's line of feed on the Muskegon River during the summer of 1997. This pattern worked well."

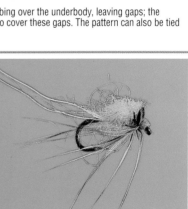

Pattern type: Spiny water flea, midge larva
Submitted by: Steelhead Connection Custom Flies (North Muskegon, Michigan)
Originated by: Jeffrey P. Bonin
Tied by: Jeffrey P. Bonin

Hook: Mustad 94838, #18; Mustad 94840, #20-#22
Thread: Cream Danville Flymaster 6/0
Tail: 2 calf tail fibers
Body: Clear Antron dubbing; atop the shank behind the eye add, tie on a small clump of egg yarn. Pull yarn up and snip short.
Hackle: 1 turn grizzly, clipped short on top

Mysis Shrimp

Pattern type: *Mysis* shrimp
Submitted by: Dakota Angler & Outfitter (Rapid City, South Dakota)
Originated by: Dave Gamet
Tied by: Dave Gamet

Hook: TMC 205BL
Thread: White
Legs/Antennae: White marabou and pearl Krystal Flash
Shellback: Pearl Mylar
Eyes: 5/64" black bead chain
Body: Creamy white Fine and Dry dubbing
Ribbing: Silver wire

Top view

Small Game Crayfish

Pattern type: Crayfish
Submitted by: Riverbend Sport Shop (Southfield, Michigan)
Originated by: Brian Hanchin
Tied by: Brian Hanchin

Hook: 4XL streamer, #4-#12; optional weight with extra copper wire
Thread: Gray UNI 6/0 for smaller hooks; 3/0 for larger hooks; or color to match body
Claws: Fox squirrel tail
Body: Fox squirrel hair in dubbing loop, trimmed flat on top and bottom of shank
Ribbing: Copper wire, medium or heavy
Shellback: Pheasant tail fibers
Antennae: Tips of shellback fibers
Weight: Copper bead

Top view

Comments: Retrieved in quick strips, this fly imitates the fleeing action of the natural. It's best fished on a long leader and floating line or a short leader and sink-tip line for deeper or faster water.

Trigger Fly

Pattern type: *Mysis* shrimp, general attractor
Submitted by: Bob's Bait & Tackle (Green Bay, Wisconsin)
Originated by: Marty Kwitek
Tied by: Marty Kwitek

Hook: Partridge Z18 WS Barbless Arrowpoint, #2-#8
Thread: Red UNI 6/0
Body: Yellow Glo Bug Yarn
Head: Orange Glo Bug Yarn
Shellback: Strip of plastic bag
Ribbing: Silver wire

Comments: *Mysis* shrimp are a major food source in the Great Lakes, and fish feed on them heavily. Marty Kwitek notes that the hook here is important—it must be stout.

Top view

Wiggle Claw Craw

Pattern type: Crayfish
Submitted by: Riverbend Sport Shop (Southfield, Michigan)
Originated by: Brian Hanchin version of Whitlock Crayfish
Tied by: Brian Hanchin

Hook: 4XL, #2-#4; heavy lead wire looped and lashed to sides of shank to provide width in underbody; Mason hard mono can be used to give added width without weight; glass rattle on bottom of shank optional. Use Zap-A-Gap or epoxy to bind underbody materials together.
Thread: Olive UNI 3/0, or color to match natural
Tail: Olive Swiss Straw, or color to match natural
Body: Tan synthetic blend dubbing
Shellback: Olive Swiss straw or color to match natural
Ribbing: Spider Wire or other polyspun gel line
Legs: Sili-Legs
Claws: Brown deer hair over long-shank bait hooks (see "Comments")
Mouthparts: Turkey tail fibers
Eyes: Burned mono, painted black, clear coated
Antennae: Sili-Legs

Comments: To tie claws: use inexpensive, long-shank bait hooks. Bend shank downward 1/4" back from eye. Tie in deer hair by the tips behind hook eye (tips should point toward hook bend). Pull hair butts back to bend, encircling shank. Bind down in two places to form joints. Clip off hook at top of bend. Soak hair with Flexament and clamp the claw portion with hackle pliers so that it dries flat. Clip claw to shape and coat with epoxy. Attach claws to body using a loop of Spider Wire through the hook eye of the claw; claw should move freely.
Brian Hanchin notes that this fly "takes lots of time to tie, but it pays off in larger fish, even in heavily fished areas. It is also phenomenal for smallmouth."

Bottom view

CHAPTER **7**

Baitfish and Leeches

Baitfish

A.J. Smelt

Pattern type: Smelt
Submitted by: West Branch Fly & Supply (Millinocket, Maine)
Originated by: Joe Brickham
Tied by: Joe Brickham

Hook: Mustad 79580, #1-#6
Thread: White
Body: Flat gold tinsel covered with one coat of Soft Body (thin formula)
Ribbing: Oval gold tinsel
Wing: Marine green Polar Flash over blue pearl Polar Flash over white bucktail
Belly: White bucktail
Gills: Red Krystal Flash
Head: Tying thread coated with Soft Body (thin formula) or lacquer
Eyes: Painted, yellow with black pupils

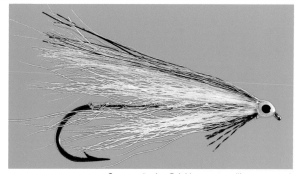

Comments: Joe Brickham notes, "I recommend coating the tinsel body and head/eyes with Soft Body (thin formula) for added durability. I fish this fly primarily for landlocked salmon. These fish are more aggressive and toothy than trout. Without the coating, even a single hookup can result in a stripped tinsel body or chipped eyes."

Andy's Dace

Pattern type: Black-nose dace minnow
Submitted by: The Fly Fishing Shop (Far Hills, New Jersey)
Originated by: Andy Sutton
Tied by: Andy Sutton

Hook: Mustad 79580, #8
Thread: Fine Translucent thread
Tail: Brown Fishair over black Fluorofibre over white SLF
Body: Silver flake Jelly Cord over pearlescent mylar tinsel
Shellback: Brown Fishair from tail
Ribbing: Crisscross wraps of Fine Translucent thread
Head: Black 6/0 tying thread
Eyes: 1/8" Stick-on

Comments: After tying, treat the head, eyes, and shellback with Loon Hard Head.

Au Sable Dace

Pattern type: Dace or chub
Submitted by: Riverbend Sport Shop (Southfield, Michigan)
Originated by: Matt Reid adaptation of Gray Ghost and Spruce Fly patterns
Tied by: Matt Reid

Hook: Traditional streamer hook, #4-#10
Thread: Black UNI 6/0
Body: Pearlescent mylar
Wing: Dark brown ostrich herl over small bunch of long, white sheep's wool fibers flanked by one badger hackle on each side
Throat: Pearl Lite Brite
Cheeks: Pheasant body or rump feathers (dull markings)
Eyes: Prismatic Stick-On Eyes

Comments: Matt Reid notes, "The subdued coloration and badger hackles really mimic a dace or dull baitfish, but this is an excellent 'anytime, anywhere' streamer."

Bead Head Darter

Pattern type: Darter
Submitted by: Riverbend Sport Shop (Southfield, Michigan)
Originated by: Brian Hanchin
Tied by: Brian Hanchin

Hook: 3XL-4XL streamer, #4-#10
Thread: Gray UNI 6/0, or color to match body
Tail: White bucktail
Body: Gold holographic tinsel
Belly: Dark gray fluff from base of grizzly hackle over olive brown bucktail over gold Lite Brite
Wing: Gray fluff from base of pheasant or grouse body feather
Cheeks: Pheasant saddle feather tied to curve outward
Head: Copper or gold bead, Sparkle dubbing to hide tie-off wraps behind bead

Comments: This fly rides with the hook point upward and imitates darters and other small bottom-dwelling minnows. Material colors can be altered to match specific baitfish species.

Bug Eyed Small Fry

Pattern type: Small fry, baitfish
Submitted by: Eldredge Bros. Fly Shop (Cape Neddick, Maine)
Originated by: Jim Bernstein
Tied by: Jim Bernstein

Hook: Mustad 94842, #16
Thread: White UNI 8/0
Tag: Silver tinsel
Body: Yellow floss
Ribbing: Silver Mylar tinsel, 16/18; counterwrapped
Belly: Silver pheasant shoulder
Wing: 2 blue dun dry-fly hackle tips
Eyes: Painted, white with black pupil and border

Comments: This pattern was designed for a local pond in Maine, for fishing in early spring when the fry first emerge and swim just below the surface. It also works well in streams, fished like a nymph with an occasional twitch.

Charlie's Smelt

Top view

Pattern type: Smelt
Submitted by: Classic Outfitters (South Burlington, Vermont)
Originated by: Charlie Lovelette
Tied by: Bill Weber

Hook: Streamer, #4-#10
Thread: Hot orange
Tail: Pearl Mylar from body tubing, frayed and clipped past bend
Body: Pearl Mylar tubing, squeezed flat to shape
Underwing: White Widow's Web
Overwing: Mallard flank, tied flat

Comments: This pattern is very popular for landlocked salmon and lake trout in Lake Champlain; it can be trolled or cast.

Corey's Krystal Muddler (Gold)

Pattern type: Minnow, smelt, baitfish
Submitted by: Corey's Handtied Flies (Yarmouth, Nova Scotia)
Originated by: Corey Burke
Tied by: Corey Burke

Hook: Mustad 9671, #1/0-#14
Thread: Black or brown
Tail: Mottled turkey wing quill
Body: Flat gold tinsel
Ribbing (opt.): Fine oval gold tinsel
Wing: Rainbow Krystal Flash
Collar: Deer-hair tips from head
Head: Deer hair, spun and clipped

Comments: Corey Burke notes that a #8 fly is the best all-around size.

Corey's Krystal Muddler (Silver)

Pattern type: Minnow
Submitted by: Corey's Handtied Flies (Yarmouth, Nova Scotia)
Originated by: Corey Burke
Tied by: Corey Burke

Hook: Mustad 9671, #1/0-#14
Thread: Brown or black
Tail: Mottled turkey wing quill
Body: Flat silver tinsel
Ribbing: Oval silver tinsel
Wing: Rainbow Krystal Flash
Collar: Deer-hair tips from head
Head: Deer hair, spun and clipped

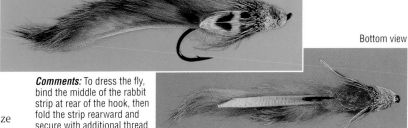

Cottontail Sculpin

Pattern type: Sculpin
Submitted by: Riverbend Sport Shop (Southfield, Michigan)
Originated by: Brian Hanchin version of Dave Whitlock pattern
Tied by: Brian Hanchin

Hook: Heavy salmon, #2/0-#8
Thread: Flat waxed nylon, Gudebrod size G, or UNI size B
Tail: Natural rabbit fur strip
Body: Blend of rabbit fur, SLF dubbing, and Angora goat dubbing
Wing: Natural rabbit fur strip
Gills: Red SLF hank fibers spun in short dubbing loop
Pectoral fins: 2 pheasant body feathers (hen or rooster) on each side
Head: Flared deer hair, gray on bottom, olive and brown on top

Bottom view

Comments: To dress the fly, bind the middle of the rabbit strip at rear of the hook, then fold the strip rearward and secure with additional thread wraps. Dub the body, then pull the front portion of the strip forward, tie off, and complete the deer-hair head. Different colors of hair can be used, or the head can be spun from all gray hair and colored with waterproof markers. This fly should be fished close to the bottom on a stout leader. It is a deadly night fly.

Fox Tail Alewife

Pattern type: Alewife
Submitted by: Nestor's Sporting Goods, Inc. (Quakertown and Whitehall, Pennsylvania)
Originated by: Kenneth W. Mead
Tied by: Kenneth W. Mead

Hook: Streamer 4XL-6XL, #2-#10
Thread: Gray Danville 6/0
Tail: Gray Arctic fox tail over white arctic fox tail over small amount of red arctic fox tail
Body: Braided silver Mylar
Wing: 5 strands peacock herl over dun arctic fox tail over white arctic fox tail over blue Polar Flash
Belly: White arctic fox tail
Gills: Band of red tying thread
Eyes: Stick-On Eyes over thread head, covered with Zap-A-Gap

Comments: "This fly," notes Kenneth Mead, "is very effective on the Delaware River system, especially with a #2 6XL hook. When water is overflowing over Cannonsville Dam and the alewives are wounded, dead drifting this fly can be deadly."

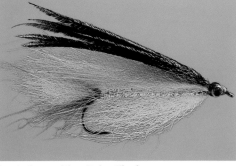

Fry Baby

Pattern type: Emerging trout fry
Submitted by: Fly Angler (Fridley, Minnesota)
Originated by: Chris Hansen
Tied by: Chris Hansen

Hook: 3XL nymph, #10-#14
Thread: Black 3/0
Tail: Barred ginger hackle tips
Body: Pearl/blue Lite Brite
Wing: Bronze Lite Brite over yellow Lite Brite
Yolk sac: Orange egg yarn
Eyes: Gold bead chain

Bottom view

Comments: "We have many trout streams," explains Chris Hansen, "that open in late winter when brown trout fry are coming out of the redds. Fish this pattern like a nymph in deep runs below known spawning areas. This fly will often catch the biggest trout in the run."

Gray Ghost

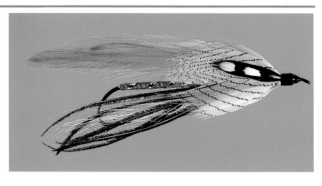

Pattern type: Smelt
Submitted by: Thom's of Maine (Houlton, Maine)
Originated by: Carrie Stevens
Tied by: Thom Willard

Hook: Partridge CS15, #4
Thread: Black UNI 6/0
Body: Pumpkin UNI-Floss
Ribbing: Flat silver tinsel
Wings: Golden pheasant crest over 4 dun saddle hackles
Throat: 5 strands peacock herl over white bucktail over golden pheasant crest
Shoulders: Wide silver pheasant body feathers
Cheeks: Jungle cock eyes
Head: Black thread with band of red tying thread

Hanch's Alevin

Pattern type: Trout or salmon fry in yolk-sac stage
Submitted by: Riverbend Sport Shop (Southfield, Michigan)
Originated by: Brian Hanchin
Tied by: Brian Hanchin

Hook: Stout, short-shank hook, #6-#8
Thread: Light yellow UNI 6/0
Belly: White Antron or Z-lon with pearl and gold Lite Brite
Back: Wood duck flank over white Antron or Z-lon mixed with rainbow Krystal Flash
Eyes: Gold bead chain
Yolk sac: "Oregon cheese" colored egg yarn looped to form bubble over tuft of orange egg yarn

Comments: Fish this fly by letting it drift naturally, then giving some short, erratic strips to imitate the fry overpowered by currents. It was inspired by Bob Clouser's Deep Minnow and Gotcha type bonefish flies. Use the heaviest tippet that conditions allow. This is also an excellent pattern for spring steelhead.

Henebry's Marabou Smelt

Pattern type: Smelt, baitfish
Submitted by: Adirondack Sport Shop (Wilmington, New York)
Originated by: Kevin Henebry
Tied by: Kevin Henebry

Hook: TMC 300, #4
Thread: White 3/0 Monocord
Body: Silver Mylar tubing
Wing: 4-6 strands peacock herl over white marabou over small bunch of white bucktail
Throat: Red hackle fibers
Cheeks: Mallard flank
Eyes: Painted, white with black pupils

Hunter's Special

Pattern type: Sculpin
Submitted by: Great Lakes Fly Fishing Company (Rockford, Michigan)
Originated by: Kevin Feenstra
Tied by: Kevin Feenstra

Hook: TMC 9395, #2-#10
Thread: Tan 3/0
Tail: Cottontail rabbit
Body: Cottontail rabbit fur spun in dubbing loop, stroked rearward as wrapped
Head: Natural deer or caribou hair, spun and clipped

Comments: This fly takes its name from the materials—the rabbit and deer that are favorites among Michigan hunters. This pattern is fished dead drift and takes both trout and steelhead.

IBM (Itty Bitty Minny)

Pattern type: Baitfish
Submitted by: Nehrke's Fly Shop (Bath, New York)
Originated by: Nate Meyer
Tied by: Milton F. Nehrke

Hook: Mustad 9671, #12; weighted with .010" lead wire
Thread: Black 8/0 prewaxed
Body: Embossed silver tinsel
Ribbing (opt.): Silver oval tinsel
Wing: Olive marabou over white marabou
Throat: Red hackle (or other red fibers)
Cheeks: One well-marked badger hackle tip on each side of fly
Eyes: Painted, yellow with black pupil

Comments: "This fly was developed for low-water use," observers tyer Milton Nehrke. "It is most effective fished downstream on a fairly long leader and 4x tippet, as hits can be vicious. Work pockets, around rocks, and edges of banks, moving the fly in short jerks and twitches. The wings should be medium full and extend about 1/4" beyond hook bend. The topping on the wing can also be tied from ostrich or peacock herl."

Jackfish Special (Brookie)

Pattern type: Brook trout fry
Submitted by: The Fly Hatch (Shrewsbury, New Jersey)
Originated by: Captain Dave Chouinard
Tied by: Dave Frassinelli

Hook: TMC 3761 or TMC 300, #6-#12
Thread: Black 6/0
Tail: Orange hackle barbs
Body: Copper Bill's Bodi-Braid
Wing: Peacock herl over purple bucktail, flanked by 2 strands pearl Krystal Flash per side, over lavender bucktail over pink bucktail over pearl Lite Brite over white bucktail
Throat: Orange hackle barbs over golden pheasant tippet
Head: 3/16" black bead
Eyes: #1 1/2 gold Mylar eyes, thin layer of epoxy over eyes and head bead

Comments: This fly was originated by Dave Chouinard on a trip to Canada to fish brook trout in lakes. It has proven effective in various color combinations in many lakes and streams.

Jackfish Special (Brownie)

Pattern type: Brown trout fry
Submitted by: The Fly Hatch (Shrewsbury, New Jersey)
Originated by: Captain Dave Chouinard
Tied by: Dave Frassinelli

Hook: TMC 3761 or TMC 300, #6-#12
Thread: Black 6/0
Tail: Brown speckled hen hackle fibers
Body: Copper Bill's Bodi-Braid
Wing: 5 strands peacock herl over brown bucktail, flanked by 2 strands root beer Krystal Flash per side, over yellow bucktail over pearl Lite Brite over white bucktail
Throat: Brown speckled hen hackle fibers over yellow hackle barbs
Head: 3/16" black bead
Eyes: #1 1/2 yellow Mylar eyes, thin layer of epoxy over eyes and head bead

Comments: This pattern can be altered as follows to dress a rainbow trout fry imitation:
Tail: Pink hackle barbs
Body: Pearl Bill's Bodi-Braid
Wing: Peacock herl over green bucktail over pink bucktail over pearl Lite Brite over white bucktail
Throat: Pink hackle barbs

J.C. Birthday Smelt

Pattern type: Smelt
Submitted by: Maine Sport Outfitters (Rockport, Maine)
Originated by: Charles W. Chamberlain
Tied by: Charles W. Chamberlain

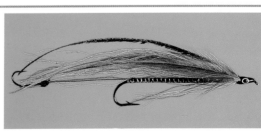

Hook: Front—8XL streamer hook, #4; rear—TMC 3769, #10; connected with plastic-coated wire, wrapped and coated with Super Glue
Thread: Black 3/0 Monocord
Body: Black thread underbody coated with Super Glue, overwrapped with transparent pearl Mylar
Belly: 4 white and 4 red strands of bucktail on underside of shank
(continued on page 104)

(continued on page 104)

J.C. Birthday Smelt cont.

Underwing:	4 strands yellow bucktail over 4 strands red bucktail over 4 strands white bucktail, all extending to bend of trailing hook. Top with 4 strands each of blue and purple bucktail extending to bend of main hook. Top with 1 or 2 strands peacock herl
Lateral line:	One strand pearl Flashabou tied on each side of shank.
Overwing:	One dry-fly quality, light blue dun hackle on each side of shank, concave sides facing inward
Head:	Black or gray thread, 1/4" long and 1/8" diameter
Eyes:	Painted, yellow with black pupil

Comments: This pattern was originally designed for trolling for landlocked salmon in Spencer Bay on Maine's Moosehead Lake, but it has proven effective elsewhere on both landlocks and smallmouth. It is trolled near the surface on light (2-4lb), long (20 ft) tippet. Tyer Charles Chamberlain notes that salmon almost always take the trailing hook and, though this is a rugged pattern, eventually the strain of too many acrobatic landlocks can flex and fatigue the wire connection between the hooks and cause it to break.

Jeff's Smelt

Pattern type:	Pin smelt
Submitted by:	Eldredge Bros. Fly Shop (Cape Neddick, Maine)
Originated by:	Jeff Lacasse
Tied by:	Jeff Lacasse
Hook:	Mustad 94720, #4
Thread:	Black UNI 6/0
Body:	Pearl Body Braid
Wing:	Peacock herl over olive marabou over sparse purple bucktail over sparse white bucktail
Cheeks:	Teal flank
Throat:	Red hackle barbs
Eyes:	Painted, white with black pupils

Joe's Baby "Bow"

Top view

Pattern type:	Baby rainbow trout
Submitted by:	Tulpehocken Creek Outfitters (Reading, Pennsylvania)
Originated by:	Joe Endy
Tied by:	Joe Endy
Hook:	TMC 300, #2-#10
Thread:	White Danville Flymaster Plus
Tail:	Chartreuse grizzly marabou
Body:	White or gray Body Fur, wrapped and trimmed to shape; colored with Prismacolor markers: back—black; upper body—green; lateral stripe—pink; spots—black
Eyes:	Stick-On 3-D Holographic Eyes

Comments: By altering the colors and sizes, this pattern can be tied to imitate other baitfish—brown and brook trout, baby bass, panfish, and shad.

Jonathan's Fury (Perch)

Pattern type:	Yellow perch
Submitted by:	Eldredge Bros. Fly Shop (Cape Neddick, Maine)
Originated by:	Kent Bartley
Tied by:	Kent Bartley
Hook:	Mustad 94720 or Partridge CS15, #2/0-#4
Thread:	Fire orange UNI 6/0
Tail:	Orange hackle fibers
Body:	Gold Tubing
Belly:	White Super Hair over green bucktail
Throat:	Red rabbit fur
Wings:	Peacock herl over gold Flashabou over green bucktail, flanked by 1 yellow grizzly saddle hackle on each side
Eyes:	4.5mm gold plastic

Comments: The series of Jonathan's Fury flies (see also pgs. 25 and 105) was designed for use in Cayuga Lake in Ithaca, New York during the baitfish runs. They can be cast and retrieved or trolled, using coneheads to vary the depth.

Jonathan's Fury (Smelt)

Pattern type: Smelt
Submitted by: Eldredge Bros. Fly Shop (Cape Neddick, Maine)
Originated by: Kent Bartley
Tied by: Kent Bartley

Hook: Mustad 94720 or Partridge CS15, #2/0-#4
Thread: White UNI 6/0
Tail: White hackle fibers
Body: Pearlescent Mylar tubing
Belly: White Super Hair over lavender bucktail
Wings: Peacock herl over silver Flashabou over lavender Krystal Flash over lavender bucktail, flanked by 1 white saddle hackle on each side
Throat: Red rabbit fur
Eyes: 4.5mm white plastic

J.P. Taper

Pattern type: Baitfish
Submitted by: Bob's Bait & Tackle (Green Bay, Wisconsin)
Originated by: Marty Kwitek
Tied by: Marty Kwitek

Hook: Partridge CS2, #2-#8
Thread: Black Bennechi 12/0
Tail: Peacock sword
Body: White flat-waxed nylon
Wings: Jungle cock hackle
Throat: Red saddle hackle fibers
Head: Band of red tying thread behind black thread head

Comments: Tyer Marty Kwitek wanted a quick-sinking fly that didn't act like a dead weight; he found the answer in a dense body of flat-waxed nylon. He says, "A rotary vise with a speed crank is best suited for getting the body material in place—a #2 hook calls for at least 2000 turns of material. You want this to be dense. The dense tapered body has a presence in the water, a mass that predators pick up with their lateral lines. The flanking material, jungle cock hackle, has no substitute. I've tried every other game bird. The jungle cock forms a silhouette which no other feather can compare to." This pattern can also be tied in orange, chartreuse, fluorescent red, and black.

Top view

L.G. Smelt

Pattern type: Smelt
Submitted by: Blue River Anglers (Schoharie, New York)
Originated by: John Murray
Tied by: John Murray

Hook: Mustad 9575, #8-#10
Thread: Red
Tail: White marabou
Underbody: Red tying thread
Body: Pearl Mylar tubing
Wing: Sparse clump squirrel tail dyed blue over sparse clump pink bucktail
Gills: Band of red tying thread behind head
Head: Black thread

Comments: Tyer John Murray says, "The L.G. Smelt was designed for the landlocked salmon in New York's Lake George but has proven effective for rainbows, brook trout, and lake trout in all northern New York lakes and ponds that have populations of smelt. It can be fished in two ways. First—slow strip, then pause, then repeat; second—quick, jerky stripping motion." He emphasizes that this pattern is best tied with a very sparse wing.

Mallard Minnow

Pattern type: Baitfish
Submitted by: The Sporting Tradition (Lexington, Kentucky)
Originated by: Rob Fightmaster and Hagan Wonn
Tied by: Rob Fightmaster

Hook: TMC 5263, #6-#8
Thread: Red 6/0
Body: 2 mallard flank feathers on each side of shank
Lateral line: Red pearlescent Krystal Flash
Collar: Red tying thread
Head: 5/32" gold metal bead for #6; 1/8" gold metal bead for #8

Comments: Rob Fightmaster notes, "The actual originator of this pattern is not known. A similar pattern has existed in central and northern Kentucky for years, but it was Hagan and myself who devised this version. The Mallard Minnow has taken trout, as well as numerous other species, in all types of water. In fact, aside from the Woolly Bugger, this is the single most effective fly I have ever fished. Consequently, it is our shop's best-selling fly year after year. The mallard flank gives the fly a broad profile, and the bead and Krystal Flash reflect just enough light to make this appear like a baitfish in motion. It's lightweight and unassuming enough to be fished in the skinniest and clearest of water. The short hook shank and mallard feathers that extend just past the bend eliminate the short strikes common with other streamers. This pattern can also be tied with chartreuse thread and pearlescent Krystal Flash."

Top view

Mallard-Bou Smolt

Pattern type:	Baitfish or smolt
Submitted by:	Riverbend Sport Shop (Southfield, Michigan)
Originated by:	Version of Jack Gartside Soft-Hackle Streamer
Tied by:	Matt Reid

Hook:	4XL ring-eye streamer, #4
Thread:	White flat waxed nylon
Tail:	Small tuft white marabou
Body:	Mallard flank and white marabou palmered Spey style; extra wrap of mallard flank behind head of fly
Overwing:	5 or 6 strands peacock herl over small bunch of gray (or olive) marabou, flanked by 3-4 strands pearl Flashabou (or Krystal Flash) per side
Head:	Epoxy (or lacquer)
Eyes:	Stick-on prismatic

Comments: Matt Reid notes, "This is a highly effective fly for stream browns wherever there is a seasonal run of salmon or steelhead. 'Skitter' this fly around undercut banks or obstructions in the river."

Mark's Smelt

Pattern type:	Smelt
Submitted by:	Eldredge Bros. Fly Shop (Cape Neddick, Maine)
Originated by:	Mark Drummond
Tied by:	Mark Drummond

Hook:	10XL streamer, #2-#6
Thread:	Black 6/0
Body:	Silver Mylar tinsel
Ribbing:	Silver oval tinsel
Wings:	2 salmon pink saddle hackles flanked by 2 dark dun saddle hackles, topped with 4-5 strands peacock herl
Throat:	Chartreuse bucktail, sparse, extending almost to inside of bend
Eyes:	Jungle cock eyes

Maynard's Marvel

Pattern type:	Smelt
Submitted by:	Classic Outfitters (South Burlington, Vermont)
Originated by:	Adapted from Steward and Leeman, *Trolling Flies*
Tied by:	Rhey Plumley

Hook:	Streamer, #6-#10
Thread:	Black
Tail:	Red hackle barbs
Body:	Flat silver Mylar tinsel
Ribbing:	Oval silver tinsel
Underwing:	Light blue bucktail over golden pheasant crest
Throat:	Red hackle barbs
Wing:	Mallard feather tied flat

Comments: Tyer Rhey Plumley explains, "This fly is an excellent early season pattern for landlocked salmon chasing baitfish in the shallows and tributaries of northern New England lakes."

McFly

Pattern type:	Sculpin, general attractor
Submitted by:	Great Lakes Outfitters (Tonawanda, New York)
Originated by:	Michael Donohue
Tied by:	Michael Donohue

Hook:	Mustad 9672, #4-#8
Thread:	Black 6/0
Tail:	Red grizzly hackle fibers
Body:	Silver tinsel
Wing:	White marabou topped with peacock sword herl topped with red squirrel tail

Comments: "This pattern," notes Michael Donohue, "was designed to closely imitate sculpin species found in the western New York area. I tie it as an attractor to stimulate sluggish fish. It is especially effective in the early trout season when the water is high and muddy. It's also effective on fall-run fish out of the Great Lakes."

Miss Julie

Comments: Developed in 1980 for Sebago Lake, this is a top pattern for landlocked salmon and large brook trout.

Pattern type:	Baitfish (dace)
Submitted by:	Sebago Fly Shop (Steep Falls, Maine)
Originated by:	Bob Thorne
Tied by:	Bob Thorne
Hook:	Mustad 3665A, #6-#8
Thread:	Black 3/0 Monocord
Body:	Orange floss
Ribbing:	Silver tinsel, counterwrapped
Wings:	Bucktail—black over dark blue dun over brown/orange over white
Eyes:	Optional

MOE Smelt

Comments: This type of tandem fly is popular in the Lakes Region of New Hampshire.

Pattern type:	Smelt
Submitted by:	North Country Angler (Intervale, New Hampshire)
Originated by:	Bill Thompson
Tied by:	Bill Thompson
Hook:	Front—Mustad 3366, #2; rear—Mustad 3906, #6; connected with braided steel wire
Thread:	White 8/0 and white Monocord
Body:	Pearl Body Braid, front and rear hooks; top of body on front hook colored with gray Pantone marker
Wing:	Gray FisHair over black FisHair over white FisHair
Lateral line:	Lavender Krystal Flash
Eyes:	Stick-on
Gills:	Red Pantone marker
Head:	Epoxy

Muskegon Minnow (Olive/Tan)

Comments: This pattern began as a smallmouth fly, but it eventually proved highly effective on trout. Tyer Kevin Feestra says, "This has become my favorite trout streamer and it is effective year-round in the Muskegon River. The olive/tan version is effectively fished with short strips. Many of my clients have fished this fly quite successfully."

Pattern type:	Sculpin or crayfish
Submitted by:	Great Lakes Fly Fishing Company (Rockford, Michigan)
Originated by:	Kevin Feenstra
Tied by:	Kevin Feenstra
Hook:	TMC 9394 or TMC 9395, #4-#8; strip of lead wire lashed along top of shank so hook rides point-up
Thread:	Tan 3/0
Tail:	Tan red fox or crossfox
Body:	Olive nymph rope or Mohair
Wing:	Tan red fox body or crossfox
Gills:	Red dubbing
Eyes:	Small lead barbell eyes
Collar:	Tips from deer hair head
Head:	Natural deer hair, spun and clipped

Muskegon Minnow (White/Badger)

Bottom view

Comments: This version of the Muskegon Minnow is best fished in long, deliberate strips. It is particularly productive for rainbows in fast water.

Pattern type:	Fathead minnow or shiner
Submitted by:	Great Lakes Fly Fishing Company (Rockford, Michigan)
Originated by:	Kevin Feenstra
Tied by:	Kevin Feenstra
Hook:	TMC 9394 or TMC 9395, #4-#8; strip of lead wire lashed along top of shank so that hook rides point-up
Thread:	White 3/0
Tail:	Badger fur with guard hairs
Body:	White Mohair
Wing:	Badger fur
Gills:	Red dubbing
Collar:	Tips from antelope hair head
Eyes:	Small lead barbell eyes
Head:	White antelope hair, spun and clipped

Nehrke's Woodchuck

Detail of rear hook and tandem

Pattern type: Alewife, sawbelly
Submitted by: Nehrke's Fly Shop (Bath, New York)
Originated by: Adaptation of pattern by Wally Allen of Corning, New York
Tied by: Milton F. Nehrke

Hook: Front—Mustad 9672, #2; rear Mustad 9672, #4, point up; connected with 40lb mono.
Thread: White flat waxed nylon
Body: White tying thread
Tail: 4 pieces silver/gold flat Mylar tinsel
Wings: Rear hook—white bucktail on top and underside of shank. Front hook—white bucktail on sides of shank over rear 1/3 of shank; white bucktail top and underside of shank at head area
Cheek: Well-marked mallard flank
Head: Black thread

Comments: Tyer Milton Nehrke explains, "This fly was named when Wally Allen showed a companion how to use his original Woodchuck pattern by stripping the line with sharp twitches—'Damn thing swims like a woodchuck,' he said. The name stuck and the fly is used extensively on the Finger Lakes and in Ontario, where it has been effective on coho and king salmon. This pattern can be used on a downrigger or row-trolled with a small sinker for lake, brown, and rainbow trout." The fly can be tied in various colors. Chartreuse and orange have proven particularly good. The color of thread used for the body should match the color of the bucktail in the wings.

October Fly

Pattern type: Minnow or fry
Submitted by: Great Lakes Fly Fishing Company (Rockford, Michigan)
Originated by: Dennis M. Potter
Tied by: Dennis M. Potter

Hook: TMC 9395, #6
Thread: Olive or white 3/0 Monocord
Belly: White marabou, one clump mounted at middle of shank, one behind eyes
Back: Olive marabou, one clump mounted at middle of shank, one behind eyes
Body: Pearl tinsel, wrapped to cover marabou butts
Eyes: 7/32" lead barbell eyes painted yellow with black pupils
Head: Olive marabou dubbed between and ahead of eyes

Olive Sculpin

Pattern type: Sculpin
Submitted by: Fly and Field (Glen Ellyn, Illinois)
Originated by: Bob Dulian
Tied by: Bob Dulian

Hook: TMC 9395, #4
Thread: Olive Danville 6/0
Tail: Olive rabbit fur
Body: White or cream dubbing, natural or synthetic
Wings: 6 variant dyed olive hackles
Collar: Olive rabbit fur spun in dubbing loop
Head: Olive rabbit fur with guard hairs removed, spun in dubbing loop

Orange Muddler

Pattern type: Minnow
Submitted by: Corey's Handtied Flies (Yarmouth, Nova Scotia)
Originated by: Graden LeBlanc
Tied by: Corey Burke

Hook: Mustad 9672, #4-#12
Thread: Brown UNI 6/0
Tail: Mottled turkey wing quill
Body: Flat gold or silver tinsel
Wing: Orange calf tail
Collar: Tips from deer-hair head
Head: Deer hair, spun and clipped

Comments: Corey Burke notes that this pattern is particularly productive on dark-stained waters.

P.B. In the Round Yellow

Pattern type: Baitfish
Submitted by: Hair & Things Guide Service and Fly Shop (Rutland, Vermont)
Originated by: Paul R. Buccheri
Tied by: Paul R. Buccheri

Hook: TMC 5263, #2
Thread: Black Monocord
Tail: Golden pheasant tippet
Body: Black floss
Ribbing: Flat Mylar silver tinsel
Wings: 2 white marabou feathers tied "in the round," that is, distributed around the hook shank, over yellow bucktail tied in the round
Hackle: Yellow

Comments: This pattern was designed for landlocked salmon and trout; it can also be tied with a red body and red bucktail. The bucktail should extend just to the hook bend, where it helps keep the marabou from fouling.

P.B. White Bugger

Preparation of marabou for marabou-tail version

Pattern type: Smelt or minnow
Submitted by: Hair & Things Guide Service and Fly Shop (Rutland, Vermont)
Originated by: Paul R. Buccheri
Tied by: Paul R. Buccheri

Hook: TMC 5263, #6; weighted with .030" lead wire
Thread: Black Monocord
Tail: Arctic fox or white marabou
Body: Olive chenille
Ribbing: Gold wire
Lateral line: Pearl Krystal Flash
Hackle: White

Comments: This version of the Woolly Bugger was designed as a flesh-fly pattern for rivers like the Kennebec and Roach in Maine, where smelt meet their end passing through the turbines. Landlocked salmon feed on the dead baitfish. This fly can be tied with a marabou tail with tip removed, as shown in the photo, to better enhance its action in the water. The lateral line is formed by attaching strands of Krystal Flash behind the hook eye and securing them in place as the hackle and wire are spiraled forward.

Ram's Wool Clouser

Pattern type: Minnow or fry
Submitted by: Great Lakes Fly Fishing Company (Rockford, Michigan)
Originated by: Dennis M. Potter variation of Clouser Minnow
Tied by: Dennis M. Potter

Hook: TMC 9395, #6
Thread: White or olive 3/0
Underbody: Pearl tinsel
Belly: White ram's wool
Back: Olive ram's wool topped with 4-5 strands Krystal Flash, clipped to uneven lengths
Eyes: 7/32" lead barbell eyes painted yellow with black pupils

Reid's Round Goby

Top view

Pattern type: Round goby, sculpin
Submitted by: Riverbend Sport Shop (Southfield, Michigan)
Originated by: Unknown
Tied by: Matt Reid

Hook: TMC 7999 salmon or ring-eye streamer, #2
Thread: Brown flat waxed nylon
Tail: A few strands root beer Krystal Flash flanked by one ginger variant saddle or schlappen per side, flanked by one olive grizzly saddle or schlappen per side, flanked by one dun variant saddle or schlappen per side
Collar: Top of shank—grizzly olive, grizzly brown, dark brown, gray and grizzly gray marabou stacked on shank; Bottom of shank—cream marabou, stacked
Head: Top—gray, dark brown, and olive sculpin wool, stacked; Bottom—cream sculpin wool, stacked
Eyes: Plastic doll eyes, posts removed, glued with Flexament into socket cut in head

Comments: Matt Reid says, "Apply a light coat of Flexament on the head after it has been trimmed to shape. This fly not only closely resembles a round goby, but it can be easily taken for a sculpin when weighted and fished in inland rivers."

Todd's Smelt

Pattern type: Smelt
Submitted by: Thom's of Maine (Houlton, Maine)
Originated by: Thom Willard
Tied by: Thom Willard

Hook: Front—Mustad 3366, #4; Rear—Mustad 3906, #6; connected by nylon-coated stranded steel wire
Thread: Black UNI 6/0
Rear hook body: Holographic silver tinsel, lacquered
Front hook body: White Polar Aire tied as throat, extending to eye of trailer hook; atop hook, 15 strands purple Krystal Flash over 10-12 strands smoke Super Hair. Then wrap hook shank with olive UNI-Stretch. Then slide pearlescent Mylar tubing over shank and bind down behind hook eye
Wing: Green Krystal Flash. After wing is applied, coat entire body and wing to rear of shank with 5-minute epoxy
Eyes: Silver Stick-On Eyes

Stormin Norman Sculpin

Top view

Pattern type: Sculpin
Submitted by: Quest Outdoors Orvis Fly Fishing Shop (Louisville, Kentucky)
Originated by: Norman Wathen version of Clouser Minnow
Tied by: Norman Wathen

Hook: Daiichi J141, #6
Thread: Black Monocord "A"
Wings: 4 grizzly hackle feathers dyed rusty brown
Hackle: 3 webby brown hackle feathers
Eyes: Metal barbell type painted red with black pupils

Comments: This fly was designed for the Cumberland River in south central Kentucky. It's fished in the conventional streamer fashion, and the deeper, the better. The hackle-feather wings on this fly are attached to the underside of the shank; the lead eyes invert the hook in the water, and the wings will end up on top. The hackle is applied in three stages. The first feather is wrapped in the conventional manner ahead of the wing, sweeping rearward. The second feather is applied in a figure-8 around the head and eyes. The third is wrapped ahead of the eyes.

Trout Hornberg Muddler

Pattern type: Baitfish
Submitted by: Theriault Flies (Patten, Maine)
Originated by: Alvin Theriault
Tied by: Alvin Theriault

Hook: Mustad 3665A, #8-#10
Thread: Black 6/0 prewaxed
Body: Flat silver tinsel
Wings: Red calf tail cupped between two mallard breast feathers dyed wood duck
Collar: Tips from spun-hair head
Head: Spun deer hair

Comments: This widely used fly has proven effective throughout Maine, including the waters of the Katahdin country and the ponds and lakes of Baxter State Park. It can be tied in a variety of colors.

U.F.F.O. (Unidentified Fly Fishing Object)

Pattern type: Smelt
Submitted by: West Branch Fly & Supply (Millinocket, Maine)
Originated by: Joe Brickham
Tied by: Joe Brickham

Hook: Mustad 79580, #1-#4
Thread: White
Tag: Electric blue Flashabou
Body: Flat silver tinsel coated with Soft Body (thin formula)
Ribbing: Electric blue Flashabou
Wing: Smoke Ultrahair over 2-3 strands electric blue Flashabou mixed with 6-8 strands blue pearl Polar Flash over smoke Ultrahair
Belly: White Ultrahair
Gills: Red Krystal Flash
Head: Pearl lacquer over head cement, then coated with Soft Body (thin formula)
Eyes: Painted, yellow with black pupils

Comments: Tyer Joe Brickham explains, "The U.F.F.O. was created for land-locked salmon fishing in a section of the West Branch of the Penobscot River. This particular section was 'discovered' by Andre Parent and myself. The relatively short stretch of river was found to concentrate a large number of land-locked salmon in the late spring. In all the trips we made there, no salmon under 14" were caught and a substantial number up to 18" were boated. The largest specimen was in excess of 20". Several fish broke off that were possibly larger. All the fish landed were revived and released. Andre and I nicknamed this stretch of river 'Area 51' as we're both sworn to secrecy about the exact location."

W.B. Pond Smelt

Pattern type: Pond and lake smelt
Submitted by: Eldredge Bros. Fly Shop (Cape Neddick, Maine)
Originated by: Wayne Bickford
Tied by: Wayne Bickford

Hook: Mustad 3665A, #2-#6, for casting; Partridge CS15, #2-#4, for trolling
Thread: Black
Body: Gold tinsel
Belly: White bucktail
Throat: Red saddle hackle fibers
Wings: A few strands purple Krystal Flash over lavender bucktail, flanked by 1 medium blue dun Metz neck hackle on each side
Cheeks: Wood duck flank
Eyes: Jungle cock eyes

Comments: "This pattern," says Wayne Bickford, "can be cast or trolled. I like this smelt pattern because it closely imitates the natural with its dark back and purple lateral area. It has been fished in a lot of northern New England lakes, ponds, and rivers where smelt are present. The fly has taken both landlocked salmon and brook trout with good success."

West Branch Smelt

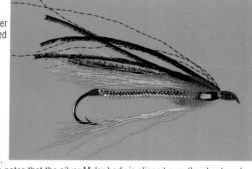

Pattern type: Smelt, baitfish
Submitted by: West Branch Fly & Supply (Millinocket, Maine)
Originated by: Bryant Davis
Tied by: Bryant Davis

Hook: Alfred Willis & Sons sproat long-shank, #1
Thread: Red for tag, blue for remainder of pattern
Tag: Chinese red UNI-Stretch, secured with red thread
Body: Silver Mylar tubing
Wing: 4 strands black Krystal Flash over 3 strands peacock herl over light blue FisHair mixed with 4 strands light blue Krystal Flash over white bucktail
Belly: White bucktail
Shoulders: Mallard flank dyed light blue
Cheeks: Jungle cock eye

Comments: This streamer was designed for land-locked salmon on the West Branch of Maine's Penobscot River, but it has taken nice brook trout as well. Bryant Davis notes that the silver Mylar body is slipped over the shank and secured at the rear with red thread. Mount the UNI-Stretch and form the tag, then tie off with red thread and half-hitch. Apply a dab of cement to the tie-off wrap, being careful to get no adhesive on the tag.

Leeches

Amedeo's Ostrich & Rabbit Leech

Pattern type: Leech
Submitted by: The Camp-Site (Huntington Station, New York)
Originated by: Amedeo J. Forzano
Tied by: Amedeo J. Forzano

Hook: Daiichi 2451, #4
Thread: Black 6/0
Tail: Black rabbit strip
Collar: Black rabbit strip from tail, wrapped
Body: Black ostrich herl, twisted and wrapped
Ribbing: Silver oval tinsel
Eyes: Chromed brass barbell eyes

Comments: This pattern is also effective tied in olive and brown.

Black Eyed Leech

Top view

Pattern type: Leech
Submitted by: Flies for Michigan (N. Muskegon, Michigan)
Originated by: Al Rockwood
Tied by: Al Rockwood

Hook: Mustad 9672, #4-#8; weighted with .030" non-toxic wire
Thread: Black 3/0
Tail: Black marabou
Body: Black chenille
Wings: Tufts of black marabou tied Matuka style
Eyes: Chrome bead chain
Head: Spun black deer hair

Comments: This pattern was developed in 1989. It is effective in both rivers and stillwaters and has proven successful for smallmouth bass as well as trout.

Cattail Leech

Pattern type: Leech, general attractor
Submitted by: Sodie's (St. George, Kansas)
Originated by: Paul "Sodie" Sodamann
Tied by: Paul "Sodie" Sodamann

Hook: TMC 5262, Mustad 9672, or any hook 2XL or longer, #10-#16; weighted along entire shank
Thread: Black 6/0
Tail: Long, soft fur from underside of cat's tail
Body: Rabbit blend spun in dubbing loop

Comments: Tyer Paul Sodamann is part of the "domestic dubbing" subculture, as he calls it, and employs an unsual material—cat fur—for this fly. He claims, though, that any long, soft fur is also effective. Color and type are pretty much immaterial. He designed this fly for the White River in Arkansas, but it has proven effective in Colorado waters as well. The fly is fished deep, with a steady slow retrieve or a stop-and-go action.

Jack's Olive Beadhead Leech

Pattern type: General attractor
Submitted by: Eldredge Bros. Fly Shop (Cape Neddick, Maine)
Originated by: Jack Brock
Tied by: Travis Johnson

Hook: Mustad 9671, #10; weighted with lead wire
Thread: Olive UNI 6/0
Tail: Olive Mini Marabou
Body: Wapsi olive leech yarn
Head: 3/16" brass bead

Plain version

Comments: This fly is designed for trout and landlocked salmon. Cast it upstream, let it sink, then use the rod tip to wiggle the fly to the surface. It can be tied with or without the bead.

Jon's Catchpenny Leech

Pattern type: Leech, large nymph, or baitfish
Submitted by: Bob Mitchell's Fly Shop (Lake Elmo, Minnesota)
Originated by: Jon Jacobs
Tied by: Murry Humble

Hook: TMC 5263, #8
Thread: Black 6/0
Tail: Black marabou
Body: Marabou from tail, twisted and wrapped
Collar: Black marabou, wrapped
Head: Black 3/16" bead underwrapped with lead wire

Comments: This fly is most effective fished upstream with a little action. It can also be tied in brown with a gold bead, olive with a gold bead, and gray with a silver bead.

Olive Strip Leech

Pattern type: Leech, general attractor
Submitted by: The Superior Fly Angler (Superior, Wisconsin)
Originated by: Gary Borger
Tied by: Keith Behn

Hook: TMC 300, #2-#10; weighted as needed with lead wire
Thread: Olive Danville Flymaster Plus; olive 3/0 for larger hooks
Tail: Chartreuse marabou flanked by yellow Krystal Flash
Body: Olive Mohair yarn
Wing: Olive rabbit strip, tied Matuka style
Ribbing: Silver wire
Hackle: Pheasant rump feather

Ostrich Herl Deep Leech (Black)

Pattern type: Leech
Submitted by: Chesapeake Fly & Bait Company (Arnold, Maryland)
Originated by: Jim Hester adaptation of Clouser Deep Minnow
Tied by: Jim Hester

Hook: Sproat nymph hook, #2-#8
Thread: Black Danville Flymaster 6/0, or to match pattern color
Wing: Black ostrich herl fibers tied Clouser style, very full; 4-8 strands holographic tinsel on each side, extending slightly beyond herl tips
Eyes: Plated barbell eyes, painted red with black pupil

Comments: Jim Hester observes, "This fly is just one of the many tied with ostrich herl in the Clouser Deep Minnow style. I have found that ostrich herl fibers are ideal as a body/wing material, especially in a leech pattern. Black is my favorite, but I also tie it in white, olive, brown, and purple. This style, tied with ostrich herl, can be adapted with various color combinations to imitate many types of baitfish also. Tying with ostrich herl fibers requires that the fly be tied very full; when wet, the herl slims down. This fly is very effective for trout in the waters of Deep Creek Lake in western Maryland."

CHAPTER **8**

Terrestrials

Grasshoppers and Crickets

Cul De Kadiddle Hopper

Pattern type: Grasshopper
Submitted by: English Angling Trappings (New Fairfield, Connecticut)
Originated by: Jim Krul
Tied by: Jim Krul

Hook: Mustad 9672, #6-#12
Thread: Camel UNI 6/0
Body: Yellow CDC feather, tied in by tip, twisted and wrapped
Legs: Yellow CDC feathers tied in by tip
Head: Brown CDC feather, tied in by tip, twisted and wrapped

Top view

Comments: Jim Krul notes, "This pattern was developed for Pennsylvania's Tobbyhannah River from late August through September. It's effectively fished by casting it to the opposite bank and pulling it into the water. Twitching it on calmer water also works. The CDC requires no floatant." Larger patterns may require 2 or more CDC feathers for the body; these are twisted and wrapped in succession. To mount the legs, tie in a CDC feather at butt using loose thread wraps. Pull the butt of the feather, sliding it beneath the thread wraps until the leg is of the appropriate size. Then secure tightly.

Hester's Foam Cricket

Pattern type: Cricket
Submitted by: Chesapeake Fly & Bait Company (Arnold, Maryland)
Originated by: Jim Hester
Tied by: Jim Hester

Hook: Dry fly, #8-#12
Thread: Black Danville flat waxed nylon
Underbody: Pearlescent black Micro Cactus Chenille
Overbody: Black closed-cell foam; red indicator dots (optional) painted with red fabric paint
Legs: Black round rubber, 2 strands per side, knotted

Bottom view

Comments: Tyer Jim Hester notes, "After wrapping the underbody, clip the Micro Cactus Chenille along the top of the hook shank. Use a drop or two of Super Glue to help secure the foam body."

Hester's Foam Hopper

Pattern type: Grasshopper
Submitted by: Chesapeake Fly & Bait Company (Arnold, Maryland)
Originated by: Jim Hester
Tied by: Jim Hester

Hook: Dry fly, #8-#12
Thread: Fluorescent chartreuse Danville 6/0
Underbody: Pearlescent chartreuse Micro Cactus Chenille
Overbody: Dark brown closed-cell foam; red indicator dots (optional) painted with red fabric paint
Legs: Yellow round rubber, 2 strands per side, knotted

Bottom view

Comments: Though this pattern can be tied in a variety of colors, tyer Jim Hester has found the combination shown here to work best. For tying notes, see Hester's Foam Cricket, above.

Kuss Cricket

Bottom view

Pattern type: Field cricket
Submitted by: The Sporting Gentleman (Media, Pennsylvania)
Originated by: Mary S. Kuss
Tied by: Mary S. Kuss

Hook: Dry fly, #10-#14
Thread: Black 3/0
Underbody: Black dubbing
Overbody: Black closed-cell foam spider body
Legs: Black Flexi-Floss (strand split in half for #14 hook)
Wing: Black deer-hair tips
Thorax: Black deer hair, spun and clipped

Comments: Tyer Mary Kuss notes, "The foam abdomen keeps this fly awash in the surface film; even when waterlogged, it won't sink. The pattern was originally developed for smallmouth and panfish on Brandywine and Perkiomen Creeks in southeastern Pennsylvania. In smaller sizes, it is an excellent alternative cricket pattern for trout. On "fly-fishing-only" waters, where the molded spider body may be of questionable legality, a substitute may be hand-cut from sheet foam. Durability is greatly improved by working a drop of Dave's Flexament into both the upper and lower surfaces of the clipped deer-hair thorax. The pattern is best fished along stream banks, particularly in areas of overhanging vegetation, dead drift or with an occasional twitch."

Kyle's Hopper

Bottom view

Pattern type: Grasshopper
Submitted by: Fly and Field (Glen Ellyn, Illinois)
Originated by: Kyle Dieling
Tied by: Kyle Dieling

Hook: TMC 200R, #8-#14
Thread: Tan UNI 8/0
Tail: Yellow schlappen tip over red marabou
Body: Tan Superfine Dry Fly Dubbing
Wing: Turkey tail section over pearl Krystal Flash
Parachute post: Pearl Krystal Flash
Head: Tan elk hair, tied bullet style
Legs: Green-flecked brown rubber legs
Hackle: Grizzly dyed brown

Reid's Irresistible Hopper

Top view

Pattern type: Grasshopper
Submitted by: Riverbend Sport Shop (Southfield, Michigan)
Originated by: Don Reid, body style from Adams Irresistible
Tied by: Matt Reid

Hook: 2XL dry fly, #6-#8
Thread: Tan
Tail: Grizzly hackle fibers
Body: Yellow (or olive, cream, gray, or color to match natural) deer hair, spun and clipped
Wing: Dark deer hair
Ribbing: Tying thread crisscrossed over front half of wing to secure to body
Hackle: Ginger and grizzly, mixed

Comments: This fly is known by guides in northern Michigan as the "Popcorn Fly." It is not, notes Matt Reid, the most lifelike hopper pattern, but it is durable, floats like a cork, and is highly effective.

Rockhopper

Pattern type: Grasshopper
Submitted by: Flies for Michigan (N. Muskegon, Michigan)
Originated by: Al Rockwood
Tied by: Al Rockwood

Hook: Mustad 94831, #8-#14
Thread: Yellow 3/0
Body: Dubbed kapok
Wings: Turkey secondary feather over black calf tail
Hackle: One brown and one grizzly

Comments: This fly was developed in 1938 for two particularly large rainbows living under a bridge on Michigan's Maple River. Designer Al Rockwood never did take those two trout, but the fly has since proven effective in waters across the U.S., in New Zealand, Chile, and Canada. The pattern is easy to tie and floats well.

Ants

CDC Ant

Pattern type: Ant
Submitted by: English Angling Trappings (New Fairfield, Connecticut)
Originated by: Jim Krul
Tied by: Jim Krul

Hook: Mustad 94840, #16-#20
Thread: Black UNI 8/0
Body: Black CDC
Legs: Black CDC

Comments: To dress this pattern, tie in a CDC feather by the tip at the rear of the shank. Twist the feather and wrap to build a rounded abdomen, ending at the center of the shank. Tie in a second CDC feather by the tip at the midpoint of the shank. Pull the feather toward the hook eye; leave a few fibers adjacent to the hook shank free to make legs, then twist the feather and wrap a small, rounded thorax.

Cupsuptic River Ant

Pattern type: Carpenter ant
Submitted by: Classic Outfitters (South Burlington, Vermont)
Originated by: Paul V. Raymond
Tied by: Paul V. Raymond

Hook: Dry fly, #10-#14
Thread: Black
Abdomen: Black dubbing
Legs: Black hackle
Thorax: Rusty spinner dubbing
Head: Black dubbing

Comments: Paul Raymond also ties this pattern in a flying ant version, using a moose hair tail and CDC wings.

Parachute Puffball Ant

Pattern type: Ant
Submitted by: Dakota Angler & Outfitter (Rapid City, South Dakota)
Originated by: Hans Stephenson
Tied by: Hans Stephenson

Hook: TMC 100 or similar hook, #16-#18
Thread: Black 12/0
Abdomen: Ginger puffball (also called pom-poms) from craft shop
Post: White Rainy's closed-cell foam
Thorax: Ginger dubbing
Hackle: Ginger

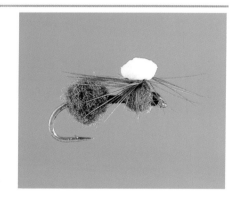

Beetles

CDC Beetle

Pattern type: Beetle
Submitted by: English Angling Trappings (New Fairfield, Connecticut)
Originated by: Jim Krul
Tied by: Jim Krul

Hook: Mustad 94840, #14-#22
Thread: Black UNI 8/0
Body: Green CDC feather, tied in by tip, twisted and wrapped
Shellback: Black CDC feather, tied in by tip and pulled forward over body

Comments: This simple pattern can be tied in a variety of colors. No floatant is required.

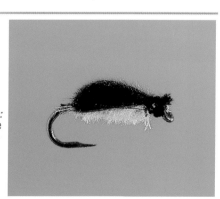

Dick's Little Black Bug

Pattern type: Black beetle
Submitted by: West Branch Fly & Supply (Millinocket, Maine)
Originated by: Don Berry
Tied by: Don Berry

Hook: Mustad 94831, #14
Thread: Black 8/0
Abdomen: Black chenille
Thorax: Red chenille
Wing: Black bucktail, stacked and clipped to length

Comments: Don Berry says, "This particular beetle appears during the first and second weeks of May. The fly is fished dry, with no movement."

Flashback Beetle

Pattern type: Beetle
Submitted by: Choo Choo Fly & Tackle (Chattanooga, Tennessee)
Originated by: Ryan Meulemans
Tied by: Ryan Meulemans

Hook: TMC 100, #12-#18
Thread: Black 8/0
Underbody: Peacock herl
Body: Black 1/8" closed-cell foam pulled over underbody
Overbody: Peacock Krystal Flash pulled over foam body
Legs: 5 strands black Krystal Flash on each side of body
Head: Peacock herl

Top view

Bottom view

Comments: This is an effective producer in Southern Appalachian waters. Tyer Ryan Meulemans notes that it fishes well in mid- to late summer, when water levels are low and fish are spooky.

Hester's Black Foam Beetle

Pattern type: Beetle
Submitted by: Chesapeake Fly & Bait Company (Arnold, Maryland)
Originated by: Jim Hester
Tied by: Jim Hester

Hook: Dry fly, #10-#14
Thread: Black Danville Flymaster 6/0
Underbody: Pearlescent black Micro Cactus Chenille
Overbody: Black closed-cell foam

Hester's Brown Foam Beetle

Pattern type: Beetle
Submitted by: Chesapeake Fly & Bait Company (Arnold, Maryland)
Originated by: Jim Hester
Tied by: Jim Hester

Hook: Dry fly, #10-#14
Thread: Black or brown Danville Flymaster 6/0
Underbody: Pearlescent black or brown Micro Cactus Chenille
Overbody: Brown closed-cell foam; red indicator dot (optional) painted with red fabric paint

Java Bug

Pattern type: Japanese beetle
Submitted by: The Sporting Tradition (Lexington, Kentucky)
Originated by: Fredrick Pfister
Tied by: Fredrick Pfister

Hook: TMC 101, #12
Thread: Black 8/0
Body: 3 peacock herls, twisted and wrapped
Legs: Black wire (or rubber)
Shellback: Coffee bean epoxied to back of body

Comments: This fly was designed for fishing the Japanese beetle "hatch" on the Cumberland River in late summer and early fall. It floats low in the surface film and accurately imitates the wide, round profile of the natural. The coffee bean is sanded flat on the underside to improve the profile assist in gluing. The back can be painted for a more realistic look or to create a "hi-vis" pattern.

Top view

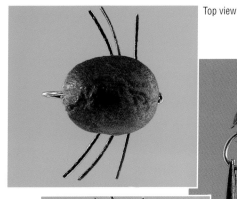

Bottom view

Pest

Pattern type: Spent beetle, blowfly, deerfly, and general attractor
Submitted by: Great Lakes Fly Fishing Company (Rockford, Michigan)
Originated by: Dennis M. Potter
Tied by: Dennis M. Potter

Hook: TMC 100, #14-#16
Thread: Black 6/0 or 8/0
Body: Peacock herl
Shellback: Yellow closed-cell foam
Wings: Dun Hi-Vis wing material
Hackle: Grizzly

Comments: Tyer Dennis Potter notes that this a favorite warm-weather searching fly.

Top view

Bottom view

Rubber Bug

Pattern type: Spent beetle, blowfly, deerfly, general attractor
Submitted by: Great Lakes Fly Fishing Company (Rockford, Michigan)
Originated by: Rusty Gates
Tied by: Dennis M. Potter

Hook: TMC 100, #14-#16
Thread: Black 6/0 or 8/0
Body: Peacock herl
Shellback: Black closed-cell foam
Wings: Grizzly hen hackle tips
Hackle: Grizzly

Top view

Comments: Dennis Potter notes that Rusty Gates's original pattern was tied with a palmer hackle and smaller wings.

Miscellaneous

Bob's Spring Creek Leaf Hopper

Top view   Bottom view

Pattern type: Leaf hopper
Submitted by: Oak Orchard Fly Shop (Williamsville, New York)
Originated by: Bob Morrissey
Tied by: Bob Morrissey

Hook: TMC 100, #20
Thread: Olive UNI 8/0
Body: Olive tying thread
Wing: Yellow Ozark mottled turkey quill, top colored with linden green waterproof marker
Legs: 8-10 fibers of chartreuse deer belly hair, spun and trimmed like legs

Comments: "I never head to any spring creek without this pattern," says Bob Morrissey. "I have had huge success with this fly on steadily feeding trout during a hatch. If a tough fish refuses a couple of pattern choices, I'll quickly switch to this leaf hopper and pick him up on the first drift. This fly has proven very productive on the Letort and Spring Creek in Pennsylvania, as I'm sure it would on most brushy spring creeks during mid to late season."

Floating Cactus Woolly Worm

Pattern type: Caterpillar
Submitted by: Chesapeake Fly & Bait Company (Arnold, Maryland)
Originated by: Jim Hester
Tied by: Jim Hester

Comments: Jim Hester finds this series of caterpillar patterns to be excellent flies in the early spring and late fall.

Hook: Long-shank dry fly, #8-#12
Thread: Black Danville Flymaster 6/0 (chartreuse for versions using chartreuse chenille)
Body: Black closed-cell foam (or colors indicated in supplementary photo)
Ribbing: Pearlescent black Micro Cactus Chenille (or chartreuse for chartreuse versions), counterwrapped

Alternate versions: Left column, top to bottom: black foam with chartreuse chenille; brown foam with chartreuse chenille; olive foam with chartreuse chenille. Right column, top to bottom: brown foam with black chenille, olive foam with black chenille.

Mouse-Rat

Pattern type: Field mouse
Submitted by: The Superior Fly Angler (Superior, Wisconsin)
Originated by: Dave Whitlock
Tied by: Matt Paulson

Hook: Mustad 3366, #2/0-#2
Thread: Black Flymaster Plus
Tail: Chamois leather strip
Body: Deer hair, spun and clipped to shape
Ears: Chamois leather
Eyes: Black beads, hot-glued to head
Weed guard: Mason hard mono

Top view

Comments: "This fly," notes Matt Paulson, "is fished on the upper reaches of the Brule River at dusk and into the dark for the large, active brown trout there."

Southern Appalachian Inchworm

Pattern type: Inchworm
Submitted by: Choo Choo Fly & Tackle (Chattanooga, Tennessee)
Originated by: Ryan Meulemans
Tied by: Ryan Meulemans

Hook: TMC 2487, #12
Thread: Olive 8/0
Body: Chartreuse Vernille, melted to a point at both ends
Bead: 3/32" faceted tungsten bead

Comments: The tungsten bead sinks this fly quickly, and it should be fished along the bottom.

Tennessee Bee

Top view

Pattern type: Bee
Submitted by: Choo Choo Fly & Tackle (Chattanooga, Tennessee)
Originated by: Brad Weeks
Tied by: Brad Weeks

Hook: TMC 5230, #12
Thread: Yellow 6/0
Body: Yellow Fly-Rite dubbing
Ribbing: Black floss soaked in Dave's Flexament
Wings: Light elk hair
Hackle: Cree

Contributor Information

Ostrich Herl Deep Leech
(Black), p. 112
Tinsel Caddis Pupa (Black), p. 69

• MASSACHUSETTS •
The Bear's Den Fly Fishing Shoppe
98 Summer St.
Taunton, MA 02780
Mail order: Flies, materials, tackle
Information and orders: (508) 880-6226
Online information/catalog:
www.bearsdenflyfishing.baweb.com
Email: beardenfly@aol.com, or,
bearsden98@aol.com
Patterns: Pink Lady, p. 27

• MICHIGAN •
Backcast Fly Shop
1675 U.S. 31
P.O. Box 377
Benzonia, MI 49616
Mail order: Flies, materials, tackle
Information and orders: (800) 717-5222
Patterns: Ben's Blue Shiner, p. 22
Borcher Special, p. 52
Chuck Caddis, p. 75
Coachman Betty, p. 10
Crystal Wiggler, p. 15
Forrester's Frenzy, p. 16
Green Caddis Pupa, p. 69
Hexagenia Limbata, p. 55
Latex Wiggler (Betsie Bug), p. 37
Peacock Stone, p. 86
Sparkle Hex Nymph, p. 39
Swimming Hexagenia Nymph,
p. 40

Dan's Fly Shop
13203 Deerheart Valley Rd.
Roscommon, MI 48653
Mail order: Flies, materials, tackle
Information and orders: (517) 275-8903
Patterns: Black Diving Caddis, p. 74
Hanson's Drake, p. 55
Houghton Lake Special, p. 11
Laur's Cat-dis–Brown Drake, p. 57
Laur's Cat-dis–June Drake, p. 57
Roberts Yellow May, p. 59
Tandy's Spider, p. 20

Doc's Custom Tackle
1804 Thrushwood Ave.
Portage, MI 49002-5760
Mail order: Flies, materials, tackle
Information and orders: (616) 327-8917
Email: docflyrod@aol.com
Patterns: Doc's Terminator, p. 35
Krom's Stonefly, p. 84

Flies for Michigan
409 E. Circle Dr.
N. Muskegon, MI 49445
Mail order: Flies, materials, tackle;
catalog (free)
Information and orders: (616) 744-1524
Online information/catalog:
www.novagate.com/~arockwood
Email: arockwood@novagate.com
Patterns: Black Eyed Leech, p. 111
Ephoron, p. 54
Rockhopper, p. 114
Super Weasel, p. 30
Tent Wing Caddis, p. 79
Yellow Stone Nymph, p. 88

Great Lakes Fly Fishing Co.
2775 10 Mile Rd.
Rockford, MI 49341
Mail order: Flies, materials, tackle;
catalog (free)
Information: (616) 866-6060
Orders: (800) 303-0567;
fax, (616) 866-6756
Online information/catalog:
www.troutmoor.com
Email: glffc@troutmoor.com
Patterns: Antron Winged Caddis Pupa, p. 68
Bob's Teardrop Caddis
Emerger/Stillborn, p. 70
Hunter's Special, p. 102
Muskegon Minnow (Olive/Tan),
p. 107
Muskegon Minnow
(White/Badger), p. 107
October Fly, p. 108
Pest, p. 117
QD Caddis Emerger, p. 72
QD Mayfly Emerger/Stillborn,
p. 48
Ram's Wool Clouser, p. 109
Rivergod Bugger, p. 28
Rivergod Emerger, p. 48
Rubber Bug, p. 117
Spent Poly Winged Caddis, p. 78

Riverbend Sport Shop
29229 Northwestern Hwy.
Southfield, MI 48034
Information: (248) 350-8484;
fax (248) 350-3163
Patterns: Au Sable Dace, p. 99
Bead Head Darter, p. 100
Cottontail Sculpin, p. 101
Hanch's Alevin, p. 102
Mallard-Bou Smolt, p. 106
Rag-A-Muddler, p. 27
Reid's Hopper, p. 114
Reid's Round Goby, p. 109
Small Game Crayfish, p. 98
Thinskin Stone, p. 88
Wiggle Claw Craw, p. 98
Wiggle Hex, p. 41

Steelhead Connection Custom Flies
514 Elsa St.
North Muskegon, MI 49445
Information and orders: (616) 744-0690
Email: jeffreybonin@hotmail.com
Patterns: Daphnia Cluster Midge, p. 92
Hex Trude, p. 55
Jeff's Deer Hair Caddis, p. 76
Jeff's Para Drake, p. 56
Jeff's Spiny Midge, p. 97

Streamside Orvis
4400 Grand Traverse Village E-4
Williamsburg, MI 49690
Mail order: Flies, materials, tackle;
catalog (free)
Information and orders: (616) 938-5337;
fax (616) 938-5339
Patterns: Simple Hex Spinner, p. 63
Streamside Mahogany, p. 49

Thornapple Orvis Shop
1200 East Paris #4
Grand Rapids, MI 49546
Information: (616) 975-3800;

fax (616) 975-3855
Online information/catalog:
www.thornapple.com
Email: thornapp@iserv.net
Patterns: The Fly, p. 67
X, p. 42

• MINNESOTA •
Bob Mitchell's Fly Shop
3394 Lake Elmo Ave. N.
Lake Elmo, MN 55042
Mail order: Flies, materials, tackle
Information and orders: (651) 770-5854
Online information/catalog: www.spacestar.net/~bobmitch
Email: bobmitch@spacestar.net
Patterns: Blue Dun Emerger, p. 43
Bob's Bead Head Flashback
Strip Nymph, p. 14
Jon's Catchpenny Leech, p. 112
TP's Hex Nymph, p. 40
TP's Little Caddis Thing, p. 79
Tunghead Lite Brite Prince
Nymph, p. 19
Tunghead Winter Stonefly
Nymph, p. 88

Fly Angler
7500 University Ave. NE
Fridley, MN 55432
Information: (612) 572-0717; fax (612)
572-9848
Patterns: Egg-Laying Early Black Stone,
p. 88
Fry Baby, p. 101
Hare's Ear Woolly Bugger, p. 24
Tan Tellico, p. 40

Perry's Trout Fly Shop
1415 E. Bayliss St.
Duluth, MN 55811
Mail order: Materials and tackle;
catalog ($1)
Information and orders: (218) 722-0631
Patterns: Arrowhead, p. 9
Duzzie, p. 23

• MISSOURI •
Feather-Craft Fly Fishing
8307 Manchester Rd.
St. Louis, MO 63144
Mail order: Flies, materials, tackle;
catalog (free)
Information and orders: (800) 659-1707;
fax (888) 963-0324
Patterns: F-C Crackleback, p. 10

• NEW HAMPSHIRE •
North Country Angler
Box 58
Intervale, NH 03845
Mail order: Flies, materials, tackle;
catalog ($3)
Information and orders: (603) 356-6000;
fax (603) 356-9760
Online information/catalog: www.north-countryangler.com
Email: angler@ncia.net
Patterns: Alderfly, p. 74
Bent-Bodied Spinner
(Siphlonurus), p. 60

Bent-Bodied Spinner
(Siphlonurus mirus), p. 60
Invaria Para, p. 62
Jon's Alder Fly, p. 77
Jon's Bubble Wing Spinner, p. 63
MOE Smelt, p. 107
Riffle Fly, p. 12
Saco River Caddis, p. 78

• NEW JERSEY •
Delaware River Outfitters Ltd.
145 Rt. 13 N
Pennington, NJ 08534
Mail order: Flies, materials, tackle
Information and orders: (609) 466-7970;
fax (609) 466-7917
Online information/catalog:
www.droltd.com
Email: deloutfitters@droltd.com
Patterns: Joe's Stone, p. 84
Olive Biot Midge Nymph, p. 93

The Fly Fishing Shop
The Mall at Far Hills
P.O. Box 923
Far Hills, NJ 07931
Information: (908) 234-2232;
fax (908) 234-9837
Patterns: Andy's Dace, p. 99
Andy's Sparkle Shrimp, p. 96

The Fly Hatch
468 Broad St. Hwy. 35 So.
Shrewsbury, NJ 07702
Mail order: Materials, tackle
Information and orders: (732) 530-6784;
fax (732) 530-6838
Online information/catalog:
www.flyhatch.com
Email: flyhatch@monmouth.com
Patterns: Jackfish Special (Brookie), p. 103
Jackfish Special (Brownie),
p. 103

Les Shannon's Fly & Tackle Shop
Main St.
P.O. Box 171
Califon, NJ 07830
Mail order: Flies, materials, tackle
Information and orders: (908) 832-5736
Patterns: Shannon's No. 1, p. 38
Shannon's No. 3, p. 38

• NEW YORK •
Adirondack Sport Shop
Rt. 86, P.O. Box 56
Wilmington, NY 12997
Mail order: Flies, materials, tackle
Information and orders: (518) 946-2605;
fax (518) 946-2497
Online information/catalog:
www.adirondackflyfishing.com
Patterns: Canary Caddis, p. 74
Henebry's Marabou Smelt, p. 102

Beaverkill Angler
P.O. Box 198
Roscoe, NY 12776
Mail order: Flies, materials, tackle;
catalog (free)
Information and orders: (607) 498-5194;
fax, (607) 498-4740
Patterns: Tobin's March Brown, p. 59
West Branch Adams, p. 13

Blue River Anglers
RR3 Box 387A Rickard Hill Road
Schoharie, NY 12157
Mail order: Flies, materials, tackle;
  catalog (free)
Information and orders: (518) 295-8280;
  fax (518) 295-7280
Email: bluriver@midtel.net
Patterns: Fast Water Stone Fly, p. 83
  L.G. Smelt, p. 105

The Camp-Site
1877 New York Ave.
Huntington Station, NY 11717
Mail order: Flies, materials, tackle
Information and orders: (516) 271-4969;
  fax (516) 271-9621
Patterns: A.J.F Ostrich BH Nymph, p. 14
  Amedeo's Ostrich & Rabbit
  Leech, p. 111

Catskill Flies
6 Stewart Ave.
Roscoe, NY 12776
Mail order: Flies, materials, tackle
Information and orders: (607) 498-6146;
  fax (914) 434-4473
Online information/catalog:
  www.catskillflies.com
Email: catskillflies@fcc.net
Patterns: DS Emerger, p. 45

Coleman's Fly Shop
4786 Ridge Road West
Spencerport, NY 14559
Mail order: Flies, materials, tackle
Information and orders: (716) 352-4775;
  fax (716) 349-2022
Online information/catalog:
  colemansflyshop.com
Email: colemans@frontiernet.net
Patterns: Brett's Light Scud Back Caddis,
  p. 68
  Brett's Scud Back Caddis, p. 69
  Coleman's Early Adult Caddis,
  p. 76
  Coleman's Hendrickson Nymph
  Oatka, p. 34
  Coleman's Hendrickson Spinner
  Oatka, p. 61
  Coleman's Male Hendrickson
  Oatka, p. 53
  Coleman's Male Sulfur, p. 61
  Coleman's Shucking Pupa
  (Spring Creek), p. 91
  Coleman's Sulfur Dun (Spring
  Brook Oatka), p. 53
  Coleman's Sulfur Spinner
  Female, p. 62
  Holt's Spring Brook Scud—
  Orange, p. 97
  Jay's Blast Off Caddis, p. 71
  Jay's Brown Drake Spinner, p. 62
  Jay's Green Drake Spinner, p. 63
  Jay's Light Caddis Emerger, p. 71
  Jay's Olive Emerger (Floating),
  p. 46
  Jay's Olive Pheasant Tail, p.36
  Jay's Sulphur Emerger, p. 46
  John's Spring Creek Pupa, p. 93
  John's Sulfur Emerger, p. 47
  Oatka Prince, p. 69
  Rose's Sulphur Emerger, p. 49

Great Lakes Outfitters
103 Cresthill Ave.
Tonawanda, NY 14150
Mail order: Flies, materials, tackle;
  catalog (free)
Information and orders: (716) 837-5226
Patterns: Alexandria, p. 21
  McFly, p. 106
  Mike's Stonefly, p. 85

Nehrke's Fly Shop
34 Robie St.
Bath, NY 14810
Mail order: Flies, materials, tackle
Information and orders: (607) 776-7294;
  fax, same
Patterns: IBM (Itty Bitty Minny), p. 103
  Nehrke's Woodchuck, p. 108

Oak Orchard Fly Shop
5110 Main St., Suite 124
Williamsville, NY 14221
Mail order: Flies, materials, tackle
Information and orders: (716) 626-1323;
  fax (716) 626-1323*51
Patterns: Bob's Baetis, p. 43
  Bob's Emerger, p. 43
  Bob's Ephemerger, p. 43
  Bob's Midge, p. 91
  Bob's Spring Creek Leaf Hopper,
  p. 118
  Bob's Trico Spinner, p. 61

Orleans Outdoor
1764 Oak Orchard Rd.
Albion, NY 14411
Mail order: Flies, materials, tackle
Information and orders: (716) 682-4546;
  fax (716) 682-7553
Online information:
  www.orleansoutdoor.com
Patterns: Baby Crab, p. 97
  Chenille Skein, p. 31
  Mark's Carpet Fly, p. 31
  Scrambled Eggs, p. 31

The Serious Angler
26 Valley Dr.
P.O Box 611
Jordan, NY 13080
Mail order: Flies, materials, tackle; cata-
  log ($.75)
Information and orders: (315) 689-3864
Email: seriousang@aol.com
Patterns: Skaneateles Brown Drake
  Comparadun, p. 59
  Skaneateles Brown Drake
  Spinner, p. 64

Urban Angler, Ltd.
118 East 25th st., 3rd Floor
New York, NY 10010
Mail order: Flies, materials, tackle; cata-
  log (free in U.S.)
Information: (212-979-7600
Orders: (800) 255-5488; fax (212) 473-
  4020
Online information/catalog: www.urban-
  angler.com
Email: urbang@panix.com
Patterns: EV Special, p. 35

Adventure Fly Fishing
2447 Battleground Ave.
Greensboro, NC 27408
Mail order: Flies, materials, tackle
Patterns: Baetis Nymph, p. 33
  Bead Head Rabbit Emerger—
  Sulphur, p. 42
  Biot Baetis Nymph, p. 34
  Biot Sulphur Emerger, p. 42
  Blackfly Larva, p. 94
  Half 'N' Half Emerger, p. 46
  Mr. Stony, p. 85
  South Fork Drifter, p. 39
  Two Tone Nymph, p. 41

Whitetop Laurel Fly Shop
172 Big Branch Rd.
Creston, NC 28615
Mail order: Flies, materials, tackle;
  catalog (free)
Information: (336) 385-3474
Orders: 888-WHITETOP
Online information/catalog: www.white-
  top.com
Email: whitetop@skybest.com
Patterns: Killer, p. 19
  L.A.S. Emerger, p. 71

Corey's Handtied Flies
RR #1
256 Richmond Rd.
Yarmouth, Nova Scotia
B0W 3E0 Canada
Mail order: Flies
Information and orders: (902) 649-2874
Email: marinacorey@auracom.com
Patterns: Black Mayfly, p. 50
  Corey's Krystal Muddler (Gold),
  p. 100
  Corey's Krystal Muddler
  (Silver), p. 101
  Dark Humpy, p. 10
  Gray Mayfly, p. 54
  N.S. Mayfly, p. 58
  Orange Muddler, p. 108

The Forks Fly Shop
74 McKenzie St.
Inglewood, Ontario
L0N 1K0 Canada
Mail order: Flies, materials, tackle
Information and orders: (905) 838-3332
Patterns: Drew Mayfly, p. 53
  Mr. Magill's Caddis (Magill), p. 78
  Peacock Emerger, p. 72
  River Ranger, p. 13
  Unusual Nymph. p. 41
  White Collar Bugger, p. 30

River's Edge Fly Shop
R.R. 13, Site 13, Box 13
Thunder Bay, Ontario
P7B 5E4 Canada
Mail order: Flies, materials, tackle
Information: (807) 983-2484; fax, same
Orders: (807) 345-3323
Patterns: Cactus Fly, p. 22
  Golden Squirrel, p. 24
  Green-butt Monkey, p. 24

  Mike's Stone, p. 85
  Nympho, p. 17
  Pass Lake, p. 20
  Philoplume Hare's Ear—Natural,
  p. 37
  Philoplume Hare's Ear—Olive,
  p. 37
  Spring Stone, p. 87
  Strip Leech—Black, p. 29
  Strip Leech—Natural, p. 29
  Strip Leech—Olive, p. 29
  Strip Leech—Orange, p. 29
  Strip Leech—Silver, p. 30

The Angler's Room
Rd. 5 Box 196—Rt.217
Latrobe, PA 15650
Mail order: Flies, materials, tackle
Information and orders: (724) 537-0683;
  fax, same
Patterns: Double "R" Stonefly Nymph,
  p. 82
  Adams—Spent Wing Parachute,
  p. 60

Delaware River Anglers
228 Davisville Rd.
Willow Grove, PA 19090
Mail order: Flies, materials, tackle
Information and orders: (215) 830-9766
Email: schwam1@aol.com
Patterns: Delaware River Muddler, p. 23
  Ken's Invaria, p. 56
  Red Quill Emerger, p. 48

Drury's Buffalo Valley Outfitters
1095 Rt. 908
Natrona Heights, PA 15065
Mail order: Flies, materials, tackle;
  catalog (free)
Information and orders: (888) 792-3395
Patterns: Cocky Knight, p. 66

Gary's Flies
363 Chestnut St.
P.O. Box 211
Mertztown, PA 19539
Mail order: Flies, materials, tackle
Information and orders: (610) 682-6255
Patterns: Gary's Alien, p. 24

Morning Dew Anglers
2100 W. Front St.
Berwick, PA 18603
Mail order: Flies, materials, tackle
Information and orders: (570) 759-3030
Patterns: Early Brown Stonefly Nymph,
  p. 89
  Golden Stonefly Nymph, p. 83
  Kid's Loop Wing Spinner, p. 63

Nestor's Sporting Goods, Inc.
2510 MacArthur Rd.
Whitehall, PA 18052
Information and orders: (610) 433-6051;
  fax (610) 433-5834
also at:
99 North West End Blvd.
Quakertown, PA 18951
Information and orders: (215) 529-0100;
  fax (215) 529-9959

Email: nestors.com
Patterns: Fox Tail Alewife, p. 101
Ken's Copperhead, p. 25
Orange Cranefly, p. 93
Trico Dun, p. 59

Northern Tier Outfitters
15 Fairview Ave.
Galeton, PA 16922
Mail order: Flies, materials, tackle; catalog (free)
Information and orders: (814) 435-6324; fax, same
Patterns: Brad's Hellgrammite, p. 95
Early Black Stonefly, p. 89
Floating Squirrel, p. 11
Mini Mac, p. 77

South Mountain Custom Rod & Tackle
Rd #4, Box 1365
Lebanon, PA 17042
Mail order: Flies, materials, tackle
Information and orders: (717) 964-3084
Email: jny@nbn.net
Patterns: Char-Shenk Special Nymph, p. 15
Improved Yellow Adams, p. 11
Jim's Retriever, p. 11
Shenk's Pearly Killer, p. 28
Small Stonefly Nymph, p. 87

The Sporting Gentleman
306 E. Baltimore Ave.
Media, PA 19063
Mail order: Flies, materials, tackle
Information and orders: (610) 565-6140; fax (610) 565-0428
Email: sportingent@aol.com
Patterns: Brookie Cookie, p. 9
CDC Puff, p. 52
Chartreuse Sword, p. 23
Early Black Stone, p. 89
Early Brown Stone, p. 83
Kuss Cricket, p. 114
Nemesis Parachute, p. 57
Wake-Up Call, p. 88

Tulpehocken Creek Outfitters (TCO)
2229 Penn Ave.
Reading, PA 19609
Mail order: Flies, materials, tackle
Information: (610) 678-1899
Orders: (877) 826-3597; fax (610) 678-4029
Online information/catalog: www.tcoflyfishing.com
Email: tcoflyshop@tcoflyfishing.com
Patterns: CDC Adult Caddis (Emerald Green), p. 75
CDC Egg Laying Spinner (Hendrickson), p. 61
CDC No-Hackle Dun (Blue Wing Olive), p. 51
CDC No-Hackle Dun (Trico), p. 51
CDC Pop Caddis (Emerald Green), p. 70
CDC Pop Caddis (Yellow Tan), p. 70
CDC Pop Emerger (Blue Wing Olive), p. 44
CDC Pop Emerger (Sulphur), p. 44
CDC Pop Emerger (Trico), p. 44

CDC Soft Hackle Caddis (Emerald Green), p. 71
CDC Thorax Dun (Catskill Hendrickson), p. 52
CDC Thorax Dun (Hendrickson Pink), p. 52
CDC Thorax Dun (Slate Drake), p. 52
CDC Thorax Dun (Sulphur), p. 53
Joe's Baby "Bow", p. 104
TCO Antron Back Nymph (Sulphur), p. 40
TCO Sparkle Wing Spinner (Trico), p. 64

Wilderness Trekker
RD 1, Box 1243C
Orwigsburg, PA 17961
Mail order: Flies, materials, tackle; catalog (free)
Information and orders: (570) 366-0165; fax, same
Email: wt@pottsville.infi.com
Patterns: Hellgrammite, p. 96
Hydro, p. 67
Tan CDC/Deer Leg Caddis, p. 79
Tan Double Bubble, p. 73

• SOUTH DAKOTA •

Dakota Angler & Outfitter
516 7th St.
Rapid City, SD 57701
Mail order: Flies, materials, tackle
Information and orders: (605) 341-2450; fax (605) 341-1457
Email: flyfish@rapidnet.com
Patterns: Biot Loop Wing BWO, p. 50
B.T. Nymph, p. 70
Carpet Caddis, p. 75
Dakota Nymph, p. 34
Deer Hair Emerging Palomino, p.92
Epoxy Back Sowbug, p. 97
Krystal Pupa, p. 17
Mysis Shrimp, p. 98
Parachute Puffball Ant, p. 115
Preacher, p. 78
Red Eyed Bugger, p. 28
Soft Hackle Beadhead Pheasant Tail, p. 39
Twisted Butt Yellow Sally, p. 90

• TENNESSEE •

Choo Choo Fly & Tackle
40 Frazier Ave.
Chattanooga, TN 37405
Mail order: Flies, materials, tackle
Information and orders: (423) 267-0024; fax (423) 267-4009
Patterns: Blackburn Tellico Nymph, p. 82
Crystal Pheasant Tail, p. 34
Dammit Emerger (BWO), p. 44
Dammit Emerger (Sulphur), p. 45
Flashback Beetle, p. 116
Foam Head Midge, p. 92
Golden Flashback Nymph, p. 16
Isonychia Cripple, p. 56
Low Rider Emerger (BWO), p. 47
Low Rider Emerger (Sulphur), p. 47
Ryan's Double Bead Stonefly (Brown), p. 86

Southern Appalachian Inchworm, p. 119
Tennessee Bee, p. 119

• VERMONT •

Classic Outfitters
861 Williston Rd.
South Burlington, VT 05403
Mail order: Flies, materials, tackle
Information and orders: (802) 860-7375 or (800) 353-3963; fax (802) 860-7375
Online information/catalog: www.together.net/~rranz
Email: rranz@together.net
Patterns: Charlie's Smelt, p. 100
Cupsuptic River Ant, p. 115
Maynard's Marvel, p. 106
Vermont Hare's Ear Caddis, p. 80

Gloria Jordan's Fly Rod Shop
P.O. Box 667
Manchester Center, VT 05255
Mail order: Flies, materials, tackle
Information and orders: (802) 362-3186
Patterns: Battenkill Lady Amherst, p. 22
Pheasant Tail Variant, p. 72

Hair & Things Guide Service and Fly Shop
135 North Main St.
Rutland, VT 05701
Mail order: Flies, materials, and tackle
Information and orders: (802) 775-5404
Patterns: P.B. In the Round Yellow, p. 109
P.B. Skater Yellow, p. 12
P.B. White Bugger, p. 109
Scraggly, p. 73

• VIRGINIA •

Mountain Sports, Ltd.
1021 Commonwealth Ave.
Bristol, VA 24201
Mail order: Flies, materials, tackle
Information and orders: (540) 466-8988; fax (540) 466-8083
Email: mtnsports@naxs.net
Patterns: Landis Leggo, p. 36

Severn Wharf Custom Rods
York River Yacht Haven
Gloucester Point, VA 23062
Mailing address:
2702 Severn Wharf Rd.
Hayes, VA 23072
Mail order: Flies, materials, tackle
Information and orders: (804) 642-1972
Patterns: Confetti Fly, p. 10
Lenexa Special, p. 12
Mr. Ed, p. 12
Red Tree Rat, p. 58

• WEST VIRGINIA •

Evergreen Fly Fishing Company
768 Locust Ave.
Clarksburg, WV 26301
Mail order: Flies, materials, tackle; catalog (free)
Information and orders: (304) 623-3564; fax, same
Online information/catalog: www.evergreenflyfishingco.com

Email: info@evergreenflyfishingco.com
Patterns: Evergreen Coffin Fly, p. 62
Evergreen Crystal Emerger— BWO, p. 45
Evergreen Crystal Emerger— Sulphur, p. 45
Evergreen Drake, p. 54
Evergreen Lime Sally, p. 90
Little "T" Stonefly, p. 90

Park Place Exxon
1 Park Place
Richwood, WV 26261
Information and orders: (304) 846-6291; fax (304) 846-6294
Online information/catalog: www.wvoutfitters.com
Patterns: Bead-Head Micro, p. 14
NB-Olive (No Brainer), p. 57

• WISCONSIN •

Bob's Bait & Tackle
1512 Velp Ave.
Green Bay, WI 54303
Mail order: Flies, materials, tackle
Information and orders: (920) 499-4737 or (800) 447-2312
Email: steelheadm@aol.com
Patterns: J.P. Taper, p. 105
Trigger Fly, p. 98

The Fly Fishers
8601 W. Greenfield Ave.
Milwaukee, WI 53214
Mail order: Flies, materials, tackle
Information and orders: (414) 259-8100; fax, same
Email: flyfshrs@execpc.com
Patterns: Bead Head Chironomid, p. 91
Prairie River Stonefly, p. 86

The Superior Fly Angler
310 Belknap St.
Superior, WI
Mailing address: c/o Dahl
6011 Cumming Ave.
Superior, WI 54880
Mail order: Flies, materials, tackle
Information and orders: (715) 395-9520; fax (715) 392-5686
Online information/catalog: www.discover-net.net/~jndahl/
Email: jndahl@discover-net.net
Patterns: Arrowhead, p. 9
Bead Head Brule River Pheasant Tail, p. 14
Berge's Black Stone, p. 81
Berge's Bullethead Hex, p. 50
Carey Special (variation), p. 19
Giant Black Stone, p. 83
Hi Vis Parachute Trico, p. 55
Lester Brown, p. 25
Matt's Golden Stone, p. 85
Mouse-Rat, p. 118
Olive Strip Leech, p. 112
Parachute Brown Drake, p. 58
Pass Lake, p. 20
Pass Lake (variation), p. 20
Peacock Bugger, p. 27
Superior X Legs, p. 18

Index of Originators and Tyers

Index of Fly Patterns